organization tips
for scrapbookers

CREATING
Keepsakes
SCRAPBOOK MAGAZINE

FOUNDING EDITOR Lisa Bearnson

EDITOR-IN-CHIEF Tracy White

CREATIVE DIRECTOR Brian Tippetts

ART DIRECTOR, SPECIAL PROJECTS Erin Bayless

MANAGING EDITOR Brittany Beattie

MANAGING EDITOR, SPECIAL PROJECTS Leslie Miller

SENIOR WRITER Denise Pauley

CONTRIBUTING WRITER Britney Mellen

COPY EDITOR Kim Sandoval

EDITORIAL ASSISTANTS Joannie McBride, Fred Brewer, Liesl Russell

PHOTOGRAPHERS Skylar Nielsen, Brian Smith

PHOTO STYLISTS Shoko Smith, Claudia Daniels

CK Media, LLC

CHIEF EXECUTIVE OFFICER David O'Neil

CHIEF FINANCIAL OFFICER/CHIEF OPERATING OFFICER Rich Fankhauser

DIRECTOR OF EVENTS Paula Kraemer

CHIEF MARKETING OFFICER Andrew Johnson

VP/CONSUMER MARKETING DIRECTOR Susan DuBois

CIRCULATION DIRECTOR Catherine Flynn

GROUP PUBLISHER/QUILTING Tina Battock

www.creatingkeepsakes.com

ISBN 1-934176-06-0

Printed in Korea.

organization *tips*
for scrapbookers

THE ULTIMATE GUIDE FOR STORING YOUR SUPPLIES

Contents

A Simple Plan

MOST PEOPLE THINK I'M REALLY organized. When I teach church lessons, I take neatly packed tote bags with all types of cool props. I have yearly school scrapbooks labeled with each child's name stacked orderly in a cupboard. I have a daily planner and a calendar I take with me everywhere I go.

But the truth is that it all starts with a simple plan. My secret to organization? I always start out with a place for everything. Once you find a way of storing supplies you really love, you'll find that staying organized is a snap—and you can spend more time scrapbooking!

That's why I absolutely love this book! It has all the answers you'll need, with an abundance of ideas for sorting and storing your supplies, including cardstock, patterned paper, cards, envelopes, scraps, stickers, rub-ons and more. Best of all, the tips are from real-life scrapbookers, sharing easy ideas that will help you transform your scrap space or craft room.

And just think, by getting your scrapbook space organized, you'll be able to do those things you love most of all—going on outings with your family, taking photos and scrapbooking those memories.

Find joy in the journey.

Lisa

Introduction

WE'VE GOT SEVERAL ITEMS IN OUR house that we don't really need—bath salts that smell funny, wood blocks that no one plays with, cookie jars that let their contents go stale. The reason for keeping them? In a word—*containers*. In two words—*cute containers*.

I can trace my obsession with cute containers back to my childhood . . . collecting Hello Kitty drawer units, jewelry boxes and pencil cups. I'd sit in my room organizing and re-organizing the colorful clips, bracelets and markers they contained. Yes, I was a little extreme. Still am. But my supplies of choice these days are lots prettier—gorgeous patterned paper and cardstock, vibrant ribbon, accents for every occasion. In short, they're everything I need for my scrapbooking.

And I've been through several storage options throughout the years trying to find the perfect container. For a while, no matter how "perfect" a storage container seemed to be, there was always a good chance I could still dip into a drawer of rubber stamps or a tin full of buttons and think, "There's got to be a better way to store this." Until now.

With this book, you'll find *systems* for containing your supplies, not just pretty packaging (though you'll find that the items provide that, too!). Find out which system works for you, then select your containers accordingly. I've even included a source guide in the back that lets you know where we found everything.

I've divided the book into four main sections: Inspirations, Foundations, Creations and Decorations. I think of them as the four main scrapping "zones"—the main processes I follow when creating a scrapbook page. If you work similarly, group your supplies into these organization sections as well—anything to make your scrap time more efficient, right?

In the process of writing this book, I think I've visited every store and website that offers ideas for storage. And I've pared it all down into the ultimate resource for your quick reference. Of course, I couldn't have done it without my behind-the-scenes creative team: Britney Mellen, Brittany Beattie, Erin Bayless, Jessica Sprague, Joy Uzarraga, Julie Scattaregia, Karen Burniston, Kelly Anderson, Kelly Lautenbach, Laurie Stamas, Leah LaMontagne, Liesl Russell, Mary Larsen and Pam Kopka, who helped me uncover storage solutions for a variety of price points and a variety of spaces.

I hope this book provides answers to your organization-related questions. That it helps you fine-tune your studio and serves as a springboard for additional ideas. That it motivates you to develop a system that will save you time and money, and that will make your scrap sessions even more productive and pleasurable.

Because, let's face it—the sooner you find a way to use your existing scrapbooking supplies, the sooner you can go out and buy more. [wink!]

Inspirations

The first thing that inspires my pages? Usually it's a **photo** that tells a **treasured story**—a memory I never want my family to forget. Sometimes it's **a piece** of **memorabilia** from an event that, like a photo, helps me preserve an unforgettable **moment**. And sometimes, I create a **layout** simply because I want to play, because I saw a layout, an ad or even a **color scheme** that **inspired** me. Something I just had to try for myself.

No matter what **mood** I'm in, these three items are sure to get my creative juices **flowing**—they're where I start my **creation process**. So, they're also great **starting points** for building an organization **system**. After all, the best way to **organize** is to sort and **store** around **the way** we actually scrap!

{CHAPTER 1}

photos

Photos

Ah, photos … the root of all **scrapbooking**. Even if you only **print** a fraction of the pictures **you take**, the images may be **piling up**, waiting to make their way onto pages. **Develop** the means to group and stow printed photos **temporarily** if you expect to **use them** soon, or use **archival**, long-term **storage** if you don't. Either way, you have **lots** of valid options.

Sorting by Date

One of the most basic and simple ways to sort photographs? By date. Organizing images chronologically is virtually foolproof and particularly useful if you create general, yearly family albums or month-at-a-glance layouts—you'll know exactly what section to choose from when you're ready to work.

Designate one accordion file, photo box, basket or bin per year, depending on the amount of photos you take. Create tabbed, labeled sections for each month. Some storage systems are equipped with slots, folders or smaller boxes, perfect for grouping photos by week, month or season. To find a specific image, you'll only need to remember when the event took place.

If you print thousands of photos or don't expect to work with them immediately, consider adding a quick index of images to the front of each section or a pocket calendar to note the year's events as memory triggers.

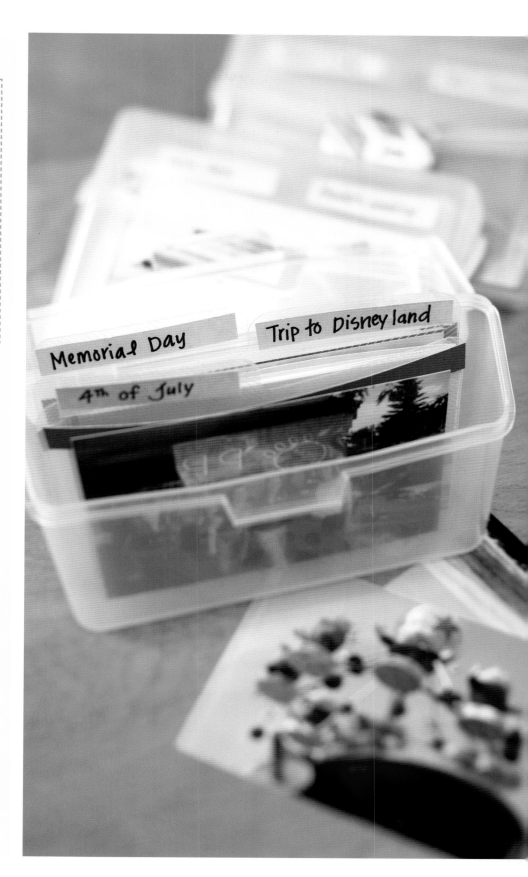

Sorting by Person or Subject

If you'd rather not sift through an entire section of family, vacation and school photos to find "that one shot" of your child's first performance, consider cataloging in smaller sections. Instead of grouping by date, sort and store shots by person and subject. Purchase one photo tote or file for each family member, then divide each into sections like birthdays, school, hobbies, milestones, candids and more.

If you scrapbook family albums rather than individual ones, gather photos by subject instead. Allocate one container to vacation images, a second to holidays, a third to achievements and so on. If you're planning to include more than one year's worth of photos in each container, be sure to date the photo backs or section tabs—when pictures begin to backlog, it will become surprisingly easy to mix one year's up with the next.

Sorting by Intended Use

With each batch of photos you print or get back from the developer, the images may fall into two main camps—the ones you'll scrapbook and the ones you won't. If you find yourself flipping past the same pictures every time you choose some to place on a page, maybe a new sorting system is in order. Weed through photos immediately when you print them, filing them into groups based on where they'll most likely be used. This way, you'll only be browsing through images you actually want to include on layouts. Divide into categories such as:

- **Layout subject.** Photos you want to use on specific layouts. Group each batch with a sticky note and add the date, along with any details to include in the journaling.

- **Album name.** Photos you want to use on layouts that will appear in a specific family, theme or mini album.

- **Display.** Images you intend to frame and showcase in your home.

- **File.** The "extras" you won't use on layouts but don't want to discard. Slip them into traditional photo albums.

Motivate yourself to scrapbook a page a day by organizing "to scrap" photos in a mail sorter with 31 slots—one set for each day. If you're worried about scratches (or the hands of youngsters), slip the photos into envelopes first.

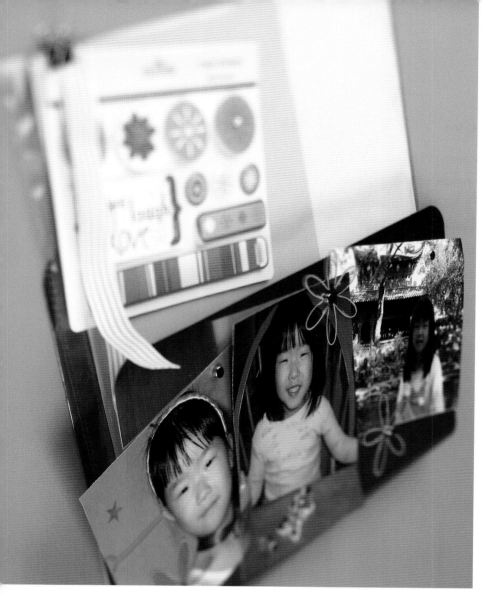

Q & A

Q: I have a backlog of photos to scrapbook—how can my family enjoy them in the meantime?

A: Instead of tucking them into boxes, put favorite photos or those you hope to work with soon on display—you'll be able to see them often and brainstorm layout ideas each time you pass. Try metal photo prongs or jumbo wood clips, magnetic frames on your fridge or wall, tabletop flip albums or traditional frames (remove the cardboard spacer in back to make room to keep a batch of pictures from a single event together). You can even scan and save images as computer screen savers or slip everything into the pockets of traditional photo albums until you're ready to scrap them.

Expert Tips from TRACY WHITE

"After making a change to the way I sort and store photos, I've discovered that my scrapbooking sessions—and the resulting layouts—are a lot more meaningful. Rather than filing images chronologically, I group them into 'chapters' within the We R Memory Keepers Photo Dock system. These chapters include topics I really want to scrapbook and fall under headings like 'Who I Love' and 'What Moves My Heart.' By storing photos according to these themes, I ensure that I'm working on what's most important to me."

NON-4" x 6" PHOTOS

Want to turn index prints into a creative goldmine? Print an extra copy and cut out the small photos. Then, store the index prints in small bowls, sorted by person or event, on your scrap table. They may be just what you need when you want to add a little extra something to your next layout—you'll have an accent photo (or photos!) of your subject close at hand!

And how to store your enlarged photos? Find a sleek document box and store the photos in page protectors until you're ready to use them!

Expert Tips from DENISE PAULEY

Now you can see how "behind" I am (and this is just one of three stuffed boxes)! I have a grab-and-go system to sort photos that lets me reach for a "packet" of pictures and immediately get to work. Here are the basics:

- As soon as my photos are printed, I sort them into groups based on future layouts. There may be too many to fit on a page or two, but I wait until I work on the layout to sift through them.

- I tie a note around each group listing the date, event or location the pictures were taken.

- Any notes on journaling, layout sketches and flat memorabilia are slipped in with the groups of photos inside the box.

SORTING AND STORING DIGITAL PHOTOS

Remember, even if you've got a reliable backup system for digital files, you should print favorites immediately in the event of a glitch. As for digital files stored on the computer, digital expert Jessica Sprague suggests sorting by:

- **DATE.** Create a new folder for each year and a subfolder for each month.

- **FOLDER.** As soon as you download your photos from your camera, copy those you'd like to print and scrapbook into a folder, named something like "To Scrap." Turn to that folder when you order prints or sit down to create a layout.

- **KEYWORD.** Use software, such as Adobe Photoshop Elements Organizer, Macintosh iPhoto, Picasa or Adobe Bridge, that enables you to add tags, labels, keywords and ratings to photos and search based on dates or keywords.

Q&³A

Q: How can I ensure my digital-photo backups are archival-quality?

A: Digital expert Jessica Sprague advocates using the highest-quality CDs you can afford (look for gold or silver alloy) and storing them upright in a lightproof, waterproof container in cool, dry conditions. Avoid writing on them with solvent ink or attaching sticker labels. Lastly, consider keeping an additional copy somewhere other than your home. For more information on archiving digital files, consult the guide written by the National Institute for Standards and Technology: *http://www.itl.nist.gov/div895/carefordisc/CDandDVDCareandHandlingGuide.pdf*.

ALBUM STORAGE

Yes, there are many ways to store completed albums other than on a shelf or coffee table! Consider stackable cube baskets turned on their sides as impromptu shelving. Purchase bookends to hold several up. Invite everyone to flip through the pages by keeping the most current project open on a cookbook stand and stashing mini albums in colorful gift boxes, hanging baskets, wall-mounted letter holders or a row of metal hooks.

Display albums chronologically if you sort layouts by year, or according to subject if you create books for different events, holidays or family members.

Negatives Exposed by BRITNEY MELLEN

With the popularity of digital photography, the days of holding new negatives up to the light are over. However, if you have old negatives from the photo lab that you've never organized, this is a fantastic solution for you—and an easy way to keep your negative strips safe and organized. Number them so that any time you need a photo printed, you'll know exactly which negative strip to grab.

WHAT TO GATHER:

- ☐ Packets of negatives/photos from the photo lab
- ☐ Photo box and dividers
- ☐ Permanent, archival-quality pen
- ☐ Small, white removable labels

Supplies *Photo box and dividers:* Paper Source; *Labels:* Avery; *Other:* Pen.

HOW-TO:

① Gather your packets of photos from the lab. Sort by year.

② Work with one packet at a time. Look at each negative strip for the photo-roll number, write it on an archival sticker and place the sticker with your negatives (whether they're stored in small sleeves or in a sheet protector made for negatives).

③ Write the same number on an archival sticker for each photo that corresponds with that negative strip. Place photos in a box or binder for easy reference—and scrapbooking. Then, place your numbered negative storage in a fireproof safe for safekeeping—if anything happens to your photos, you'll have a backup!

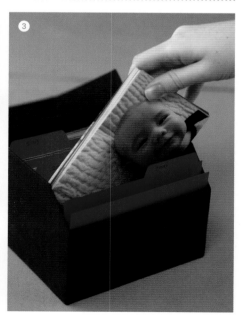

{CHAPTER 2}

memorabilia

Memorabilia

There are many ways to add **meaning** to your layouts—favorite photos, journaling and **memorabilia**, the letters, **souvenirs** and other **morsels** you **collect** along the journey of life. **Preserve** them in containers that will keep **one-of-a-kind** items archivally safe and **prevent** delicate pieces from getting wrinkled or **damaged**.

Sorting by Owner

If you've got a large family, you've got a large memorabilia collection. Over the years, all of the vacation mementos, school projects, sports awards, birthday cards and assorted keepsakes are bound to start piling up.

Separate according to family member to simplify sorting and searching—you can immediately head to the right container when looking for ephemera to use on a layout. Obtain one acid-free album per person to stow documents, notes, schoolwork and other flat items and one larger box each for dimensional trinkets. To keep storage as compact as possible, house each album inside each corresponding box, along with a smaller container or padded envelope to help locate and protect smaller pieces. Attach a list with the person's name and with the dates and descriptions of each item contained within.

Sorting by Importance or Value

All memorabilia is not created equal. While some (such as historical documents, wedding keepsakes and family heirlooms) are priceless with sentimental value, others (such as ticket stubs, travel brochures, playbills and receipts) are probably a little less so. Let the difference determine the storage method and its archival safety.

Sort items by their importance and worth, measured not only in monetary terms, but in meaning as well. Store irreplaceable pieces in archival files, closed containers or even within a fireproof safe. Less critical ephemera that you intend to scrapbook immediately can be organized in an accordion file or binder, displayed in a shadow box, or housed in a postcard rack or on a French memory board. *(For additional tips on archival storage, see the Q&A on page 39.)*

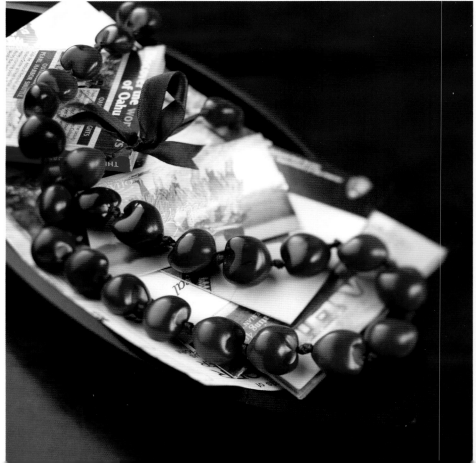

Sorting by Weight and Dimension

Memorabilia and ephemera come in many sizes, from a tiny button off a baby sweater to a towering championship trophy. Storing large with small, fragile with sturdy, or light with heavy can pose problems for the safety of your keepsakes. Group pieces by weight and dimension to make access easier and to keep delicate items from being crushed or trinkets from being lost.

Try photo boxes for smaller bits and pieces (with miniscule items separated in envelopes or tins). Use archival albums or accordion files for newspaper clippings, certificates and brochures. Turn large, lidded bins into oversized memorabilia storage. If you won't need to access the mementos frequently, store them in flat boxes that can be slipped under the bed, in the closet or behind other items. Add photos of the contents to the lid or sides so you won't have to open the containers to see what's inside.

DISPLAYING MEMORABILIA

Sometimes the best scrapbook inspiration comes when we least expect it. But you can help it come faster when your memorabilia is on display—and a constant reminder to think of a way to scrapbook it when something on the television or in a magazine establishes an inspirational connection, such as when an ad provides the right design or color scheme for your brochures from last summer's vacation. But you can't display all your memorabilia, so how do you choose what to feature? Consider these ideas:

- If you have several events you're wanting to scrap, display one—and only one—"keynote" item from each event.

- Display the item you think will be hardest to scrap. Tickets and brochures may be easy to scrapbook, for example, but the crocheted handkerchief you picked up as a souvenir may be the item causing scrapper's block. Keep the tickets and brochures in your memorabilia files and display the handkerchief in view.

- Create a hierarchy of importance. If not all items will fit on your magnetic board, keep a file on or near the side where items can be stacked behind each other. When you scrapbook an item from the board, remove the front item from the file and post it in the open place. Then, you'll have all the items handy, but only the most important will get a prime spot.

Expert Tips from REBECCA SOWER

One of the spaces on Rebecca Sower's oak library bookshelf houses a display of ephemera and memorabilia. Hear more about the system she turns to for items and inspiration:

- A spring-style curtain rod sits inside one of the bookshelf compartments, braced on the side panels.

- Everything from envelopes and library pockets to playing cards are sorted by type, then hung on rings that slide back and forth effortlessly.

- Keeping items out in the open helps Rebecca remember what's available to use on each project.

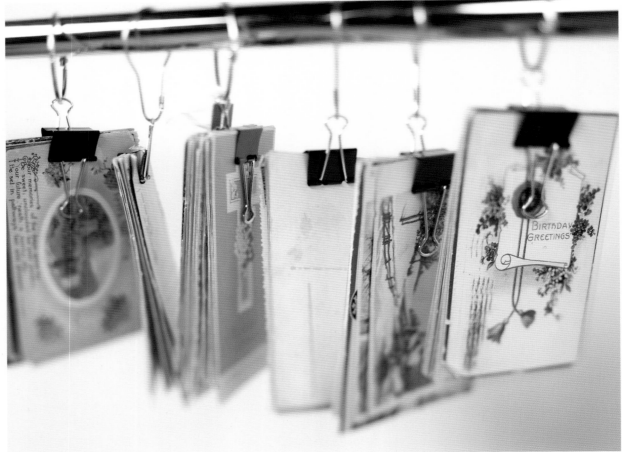

Q&A

Q: I know it's vital that photos and memorabilia are kept in archival-quality containers, but what about the rest of my supply stash?

A: If you're planning on storing supplies long-term and are concerned about archival safety, consider these additional safety factors:

- **DOUBLE-CHECK PLASTICS.** Avoid PVC (polyvinyl-chloride) containers and look for units manufactured with polypropylene. Most scrapbook-related storage products will include details about their material composition.

- **DRY COMPLETELY.** If you're using containers previously used elsewhere in your home, be sure they're washed and completely dry before adding contents. (For ideas on getting more from your current containers, see page 92.)

- **BLOCK DUST AND SUN.** Avoid open containers if your house seems particularly dusty or if products will sit in direct sunlight. Some manufacturers even offer lightweight covers for open storage units.

- **AVOID ACID MIGRATION.** Store memorabilia, especially newspapers, away from other items. You may wish to treat documents with an acid-neutralizing spray before storing or adding to a layout.

- **WATCH YOUR HANDS.** Oil and dirt are easily transferred from your hands to your keepsakes—and their containers. Use pairs of print or film-handling gloves if you want to be extra careful.

Q&A

Q: After vacation, I have all sorts of brochures and tidbits stuffed in my suitcase, purse and souvenir bags. Is there a better way to collect and protect memorabilia I gather when I'm away from home?

A: When you're taking a trip, pack a few flat boxes that will fit in your purse. Use them to hold bits and pieces you'll want to include in vacation albums. The boxes will help you organize items and prevent wrinkles. Use them to store business cards from unique shops, takeout menus from favorite restaurants, receipts and tags, postcards and brochures, snippets like shells from the beach, photos, and notes for journaling. If you're worried about losing a separate container, find a photo album, planner or business case with straps and let it double as your purse.

Expert Tips from KELLY ANDERSON

"I keep my favorite bits of ephemera displayed in a vintage postcard carousel from Pottery Barn. I tend to use what I can see, and the carousel keeps all the items I'd like to use in my artwork at the ready. I'm happy that it's not only useful but also a decorative way to store postcards from favorite destinations and sentimental greeting cards I've received."

BULKY MEMORABILIA

Scrapbooks are perfect for preserving memories . . . but not so perfect for holding any weighty or dimensional items that go along with them. If you've got a collection of large school projects, souvenirs and keepsakes, include them on your layouts by:

■ **SCANNING.** Capture an image to output on your printer. If you can't close the lid all the way over your scanner, drape a towel over it while you scan to even out the lighting.

■ **PHOTOGRAPHING.** Take a few photos of the object. Isolate it against a neutral background, or include other related props in the background to help you tell the story of the item.

■ **INDEXING.** Store all dimensional memorabilia pieces in a central place and add a small ID tag to each. Refer to the tag numbers on your layouts as a reference. If you number them chronologically as you go, you won't have to create separate storage containers for memorabilia sorted by person, event and so on.

Case Closed by BRITNEY MELLEN

Pack up a colorful photo-labeled memorabilia box for each family member. It's the perfect home for artwork, crafts, trinkets and any other items that are too bulky to fit between the pages of your scrapbook. Who says "you can't take it with you"?

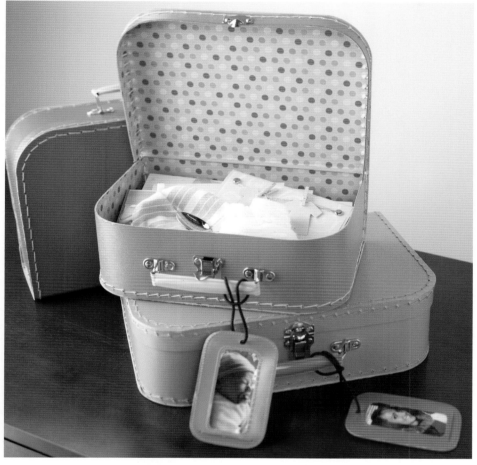

WHAT TO GATHER:

☐ Luggage tag

☐ Memorabilia

☐ Mini suitcase or box

☐ Wallet-size photo for each family member

Supplies *Suitcases:* Paper Source; *Luggage tags:* Lug.

HOW-TO:

① Sort memorabilia into piles for each family member.

② Label sorted items with dates if necessary and place each person's items into his or her memorabilia box.

③ Insert a photo into each luggage tag. Attach tags to corresponding memorabilia boxes.

Optional: At the end of each year, have family members sort through last year's mementos, keeping the best and recycling the rest. But remember, you aren't limited to one box per person—stack 'em up for a cute (and meaningful) shelf display.

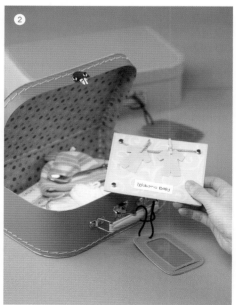

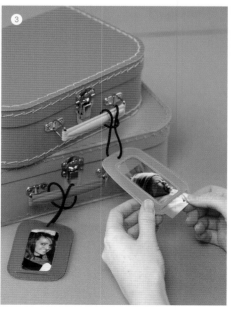

{CHAPTER 3}

ideas

Ideas

Inspiration is **everywhere**. You never know when you'll **discover** a **trend** or **technique** in a scrapbooking **magazine**, a color combination in a clothing ad, or a **title** on a billboard. Don't let these **snippet**s slip away! Jot them down or **compile** an **idea file** where they can motivate you and trigger **additional** ideas.

- Books
- Loose items torn from fashion, decor or other magazines
- Magazines
- Photos of cool sights, signs or objects
- Product packaging
- Swatches (texture, color, etc.)
- Tags, cards or labels that inspire you

Ideas to Scraplift Directly

There are a few different levels of ideas out there . . . and more than a few ways to store them. One type of inspiration is ideas you can use directly as they are—designs and elements that you spot in a scrapbooking publication and instantly want to use to suit your style and layout. Clip the tidbits and store them in a system on your desk to assist when you're in need of a creative boost. Or devise a color-coded system of sticky notes, tabs or bookmarks to flag favorite ideas if you'd rather keep magazines and books intact. Clippings can serve as springboards for future pages. Separate them into helpful categories (and possible subcategories) like:

- **Ads** (colors, designs, layout samples)
- **Basics** (accents, borders, photo mats, title blocks, corners)
- **Color combinations**
- **Journaling** (interesting writing styles or designs)
- **Layouts** (design, number of photos, subjects, themes)
- **Photos** (points of view, lighting, overall feel)
- **Techniques and textures**
- **Tips and tricks**
- **Titles and quotes**

Ideas to Inspire

Another type of inspiration comprises ideas to use for brainstorming—snippets that might lead to a new concept for a layout topic, design, background, photo, color combination or page element. Be alert because you never know when these morsels will grab you . . . or where they'll come from. Elements can catch your eye while you're taking a walk, shopping, doing laundry, eating dinner, reading a bedtime story or sifting through junk mail.

Indirect inspiration—that you can tear out, photograph or jot down—is great to display on magnet or cork boards, photo clips, dry-erase boards or clipboards, where you'll see them repeatedly, allowing ideas to percolate. When you're ready to place the tidbits into a binder or box, try sorting into groups like:

- Color
- Design
- Photography
- Subjects and stories
- Texture
- Typography

Keep the ideas more generic on this one, so the springboards can take you to even more creative places in your scrapbooking process.

EYE CANDY

Expert Tips from BRENDA ARNALL

While Brenda Arnall can't help but covet some of the "newer, more colorful" magazine holders, she's hanging onto the generic versions purchased at an office-supply store that suit her just fine. Here's what she enjoys about the traditional storage:

- Vertical storage makes it easy to read the titles. It also keeps everything tidy.

- She places magazines in chronological order, which makes it simple to locate the oldest issues when it's time to sort and purge her stash.

- When the containers become a little too stuffed, she gets rid of the oldest issues, looking through them first to save any timeless and inspiring ideas.

Expert Tips from JOY UZARRAGA

"These days, my inspiration comes from catalogs and magazines. I keep a binder for the ideas—I simply tear the pages out and store them in page protectors. When I need a little motivation, I just flip through the pages. If I happen to use one of the ideas, I'll throw away that page to make room for a newer image."

Ideas for Creative Play

Now, possibly the most interesting kind of inspiration comes from ideas to play with—tips, textures and techniques you spot in magazines, stores, nature or your own home that you can't wait to imitate, re-create or expand upon. Carry a small notebook, camera or batch of index cards wherever you go—a place to sketch or write notes whenever inspiration strikes. Stow these ideas in a notebook, binder or album, preferably one with pockets or slots for clippings and sturdy paper to actually experiment with the ideas. Your idea storage can become an art journal of sorts—a place to try out, rule out and develop new techniques. Possible categories (and subcategories) can include the following:

- Lettering (handwriting, hand-cutting, using computer fonts)

- Materials (fabric, ribbon, metal, paper, transparencies, wire)

- Media (paint, chalk, rub-on, ink, dye, watercolor, glaze, finish)

- Photography (angles, lighting, altering)

- Techniques and tools (stamping, punching, embossing, distressing, folding, layering, cutting, stitching, doodling)

- Textures (building up, pressing in, layering materials)

- Timesavers

Q & A

Q: I'm great at starting idea files, but how can I remind myself to update and actually use them?

A: Keep your ideas where you'll notice them and absorb the inspiration: Alter a book to match your decor and keep it on your nightstand or coffee table, buy a tin or Rolodex to keep in your kitchen, pin groupings to magnet boards near your door, or hang batches of tags, envelopes or small notebooks above your desk. Seeing the system is crucial to actually using it.

Keep it fun as well. Don't just add clippings and quotes to the book—play in it, too. You're bound to turn to the file often if you use it as a place to experiment with new skills and textures.

MORE NOTEBOOK SOLUTIONS

We all have them—notebooks where we can store everything we think of related to scrapbooking. But if you find yourself avoiding your idea notebook when you actually need an idea, perhaps it's time to rethink the system.

Instead of keeping sketches with color palettes and everything else, keep a separate notebook for each (especially when they're used at home and you don't have to carry multiples around). For example, if a few scrapbook designers catch your eye, devote mini idea collections to each one. Sometimes dividing truly will help you conquer.

Expert Tips from TRACY WHITE

"All of my scrapbooking ideas are stored on the pages of my Memory Dock Creative Planner. I've got a section for sketches and another for future layout ideas. The book is also the perfect place for quotes, lyrics and a reference list of the issues, titles and page numbers of layouts in magazines and idea books that I find inspiring."

GO DIGITAL

If your scrap space is filling up too quickly with supplies (and whose isn't!), consider keeping your "inspirational ideas" storage on the computer. You'll clear up extra room for more supplies (shopping, anyone?), and you'll be able to do quick searches to find what you need. Consider keeping an idea file with the following categories:

- LAYOUTS (images scanned from magazines, saved from online galleries, shared from digital scrapbookers)

- PHOTOS (cool photos you want to copy, favorite photos you want to scrapbook soon)

- TECHNIQUES (step-by-step instructions found online or scanned from magazines, links to or downloads of technique videos)

- VARIOUS IDEAS (screen shots of inspiring web pages, scanned items from your current idea storage)

Expert Tips from JESSICA SPRAGUE

"I have three types of idea books: scrapbook, graphic/decor design and how-to (for things like Photoshop). Each category makes up a stack on my bookshelf, and most of the books are peppered with sticky notes to flag favorite ideas. When I need help with a technique, I access the 'how-to' stack. When I'm feeling mojo-less, I head to the 'design' stack. Each pile fulfills a need for me."

HANDCRAFTED PROJECTS FOR YOUR HOME

LAST-MINUTE FABRIC GIFTS

HOW TO PHOTOGRAPH YOUR BABY

drop dead Photography Techniques

Digital Family Album Basics

The New Book of Image Transfer

PHOTOGRAPHY FOR SCRAPBOOKERS

HOW TO PHOTOGRAPH YOUR FAMILY

How-to

Inspiration Station by BRITNEY MELLEN

Transform any frame into a catchall for inspirational tidbits you don't want to file away. Pick a fabric covering that coordinates with your home decor. Hang your inspiration board wherever you usually create, and watch your creativity increase!

WHAT TO GATHER:

☐ Fabric (3" larger than the foam core on each side)

☐ Foam core at least ½" thick (cut to fit inside desired frame)

☐ Frame

☐ Staple gun

Supplies *Frame and fabric:* Jo-Ann Stores; *Foam core:* Elmer's; *Other:* Heavy-duty staples.

HOW-TO:

① Tightly stretch fabric over foam core.

② Use a staple gun to secure fabric to back of foam core.

③ Place the covered board inside the frame.

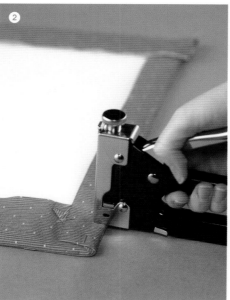

Foundations

Once I **know** what I want to scrap (i.e., the photos, the story, the memorabilia), **99 percent** of the time I head **straight** to my **paper storage**. Who can resist the beautiful papers and cardstock we scrappers get to **choose** from? **Certainly** not me . . . **which means** it can pile up quickly.

Without a good organization system for my paper and cardstock, these **yummy papers** (and kits!) would be so **disorganized** I'd probably never want to scrap— who'd want to sift through **all of it** to find just the **right hue**? Again, not me. But with my **loose** paper and scraps **organized** and my preplanned and **store-bought** kits all in order, getting **started** is a breeze— and **energizing**! And if you're a card-maker, you'll find the same concept **applies** for all of your **card supplies**, too.

Once you find the **right system** for you on the **following** pages, jump in and get organized! A **little** time spent organizing **up front** means **more time** for scrapping in the future instead of **searching** for just the right **paper**.

{CHAPTER 4}

cardstock, scraps &³ patterned paper

Cardstock, Scraps & Patterned Paper

As staples of scrapbooking, **cardstock** and patterned paper are often the first **products** a scrapbooker selects for a layout. A good **storage system** will allow you to **coordinate** colors and designs quickly, while preventing paper damage, such as crumpled and bent edges. The **container** you choose can also **save you money** in the long run, because it will help you remember—and thereby use—your **paper scraps**.

Sorting by Color

The best way to sort cardstock and papers? Simple. Let the way you select papers for a page drive the way you store them. If you most often match the background to the photos and the patterned paper to the background, for example, sort sheets by color.

Decide if you'd rather store everything horizontally or vertically, in stationary drawers and files, or in portable totes and rolling carts. Then designate one section per color or shade—if the container you chose doesn't have enough slots, combine similar colors, like greens and blues, oranges and yellows, and so on.

Patterned paper can sit in the same container as coordinating cardstock or in an entirely different unit. Scraps, as well as small-format cardstock and patterned paper, can be kept in baggies or envelopes alongside whole sheets or stored in their own containers.

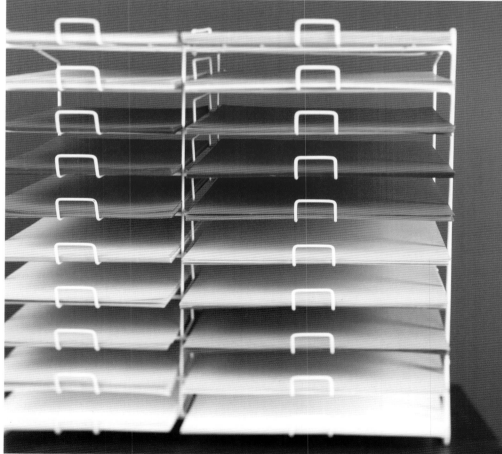

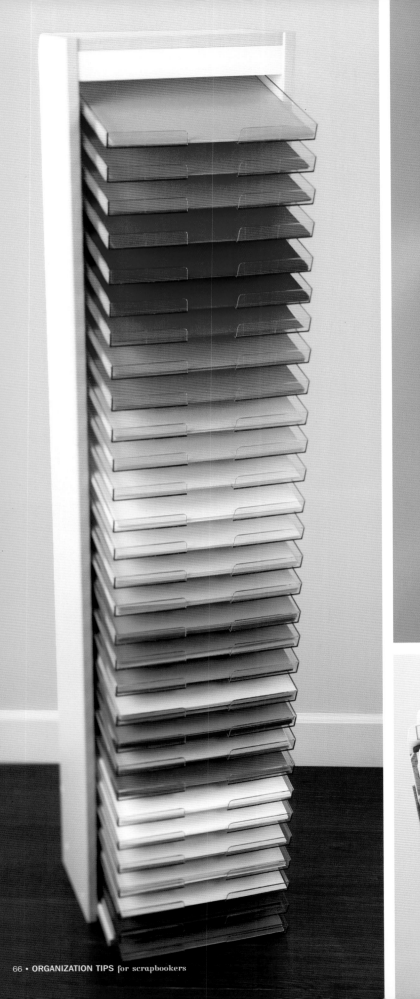

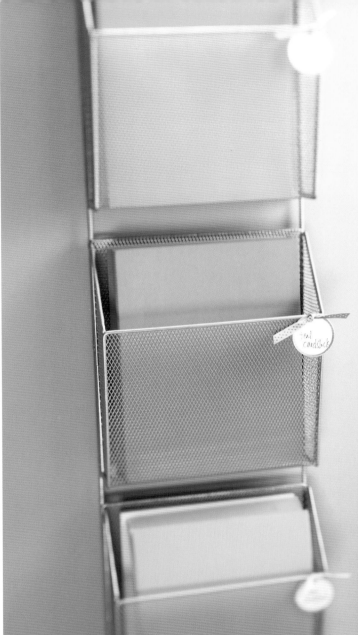

Sorting by Manufacturer

Sort by manufacturer if these qualities describe you: First, when you stroll through a scrapbook store or browse online for cardstock and paper, you head straight to the section dedicated to your favorite paper lines. Second, when you see pages in a scrapbook publication, you can identify the product manufacturer even before you check the supply list. Third, you choose one company's merchandise over another because you like the style and feel of the designs.

If you're especially familiar with and partial to specific designers and looks, then separating papers by manufacturer might be the best system for you. Sorting in this manner makes combining items within the same product lines, selecting paper to match the mood of your layout, and finding exact cardstock and patterned paper matches a breeze. If the sheets from some companies begin to overflow from their section, drawer or file, subdivide by collection, designer or release date. Conversely, if you have too few to justify an entire slot, combine papers from manufacturers that have a similar "feel," or alphabetize them by company name.

Sorting by Theme or Design

If you predominantly scrapbook event-based layouts, design single-subject mini albums or just love themed patterned paper, you'll want to sort your papers by design. Allocate a pouch, drawer or hanging file for each type, starting with broad categories like holidays, school, celebrations, sports and nature. If one section is too stuffed and makes locating specific images a chore, subdivide it—break holidays into Christmas, Easter and Valentine's Day, for example.

Dividing by design is also a helpful way to separate decorative patterned papers, particularly if you mix and match patterns or use them to create a certain feel for each layout. Try sections such as solids, stripes, dots and circles, plaids and squares, doodles, abstract, flowers and text. Or classify by overall style with labels—cute, elegant, distressed, vintage, graphic, feminine, masculine, artistic and simple. Remember, you're developing a "flow" for materials selection, so your system should be based on what you primarily "look for" when choosing papers for your pages.

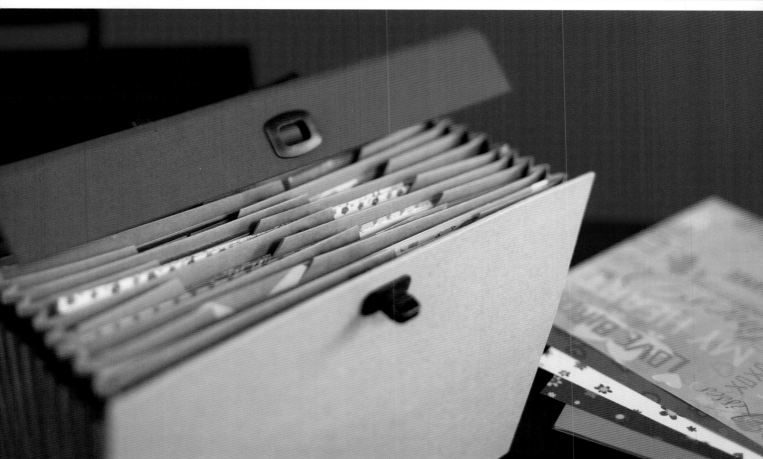

Expert Tips from DENISE PAULEY

I've tried storing scraps in everything from accordion totes to envelopes to hanging files. But this system is the keeper for me: storing scraps in a 12" x 12" three-drawer Sterilite unit—one drawer for pinks and purples, a second for blues and greens, and a third for yellows, browns and oranges. It works because:

- The unit fits 12" x 12" paper, so I don't have to trim longer pieces to fit. In addition, the drawers are easy to remove and carry to my workspace.

- It's so painless to open the drawer and add scraps, I'm not tempted to toss them out when I'm feeling lazy.

- Because I have multiple colors and styles grouped together, I may be searching for one piece but then find another that suits my layout better.

Expert Tips from KELLY LAUTENBACH

"I store smaller cardstock and patterned papers in a little caddy that's both decorative and functional. It not only adds a charming touch to my desk, but it also keeps sheets out so I can remember to use them on smaller projects. I like that they're sitting out as a constant reminder."

CONTAINER SIZING

If you want storage that's an exact fit for different sizes of cardstock, paper or other supplies (to prevent any unused space), you'll want to check out containers that come in several sizes. But you'll also want to avoid buying containers that are too large or too small.

Avoid repeated trips to the store with this organization tip: If a container's interior dimensions aren't listed on the label, don't just eyeball it, especially if you want a good match for non-standard items like 6" x 6" cardstock. Take a sample piece along or trace and cut a "model" of unusually sized items and place them inside the container at the store as a test run. Keeping a list of exact measurements in a notebook and a tiny tape measure in your bag will also prove handy.

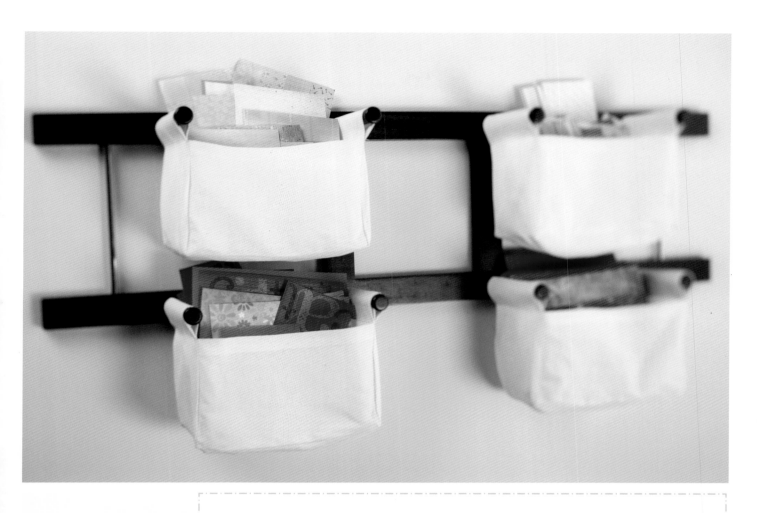

SCRAP SAVVY

We toss scraps into a bin with the best of intentions . . . but if that bin turns into a black hole, there's no point hanging onto the heap. Make using scraps more convenient by only keeping what you'll want to use and buy.

Try these ideas:

- **TRIMMING.** Make scraps appealing—trim torn, punched or bent edges before filing.

- **SIZING.** If you typically need scraps for photo mats and letter blocks or strips for punching, consider precutting scraps to those sizes and designating a bin specifically for each size.

- **SORTING.** File scraps with the same system you use for cardstock and patterned paper to help you locate colors and designs quickly.

- **VIEWING.** Situate your scrap container where you'll consistently check it.

- **COMBINING.** If you always bypass the scrap bin, store pieces in folders next to your full sheets of cardstock and paper.

- **REMEMBERING.** Routinely sift through your scraps first thing when making cards and gift tags, mini albums, die cuts, punches, labels, collages and accents—before you ever look through your full-paper storage.

Q&A

Q: I purchased a paper rack that's larger than I need. What else can I use it for?

A: Buying cardstock and paper storage that fits your space (rather than your current stash) is a great idea since it gives you room to grow. In the meantime, use extra shelves to hold magazines and idea books; sticker, rub-on and chipboard sheets; large scraps directly above or below full-sized pieces of paper; and even rubber or foam stamps layered in acrylic box frames. If the paper rack features metal rungs, you can also hang bags of embellishments, product packaging and ribbon cards to the sides with S-hooks, binder rings or ribbon ties.

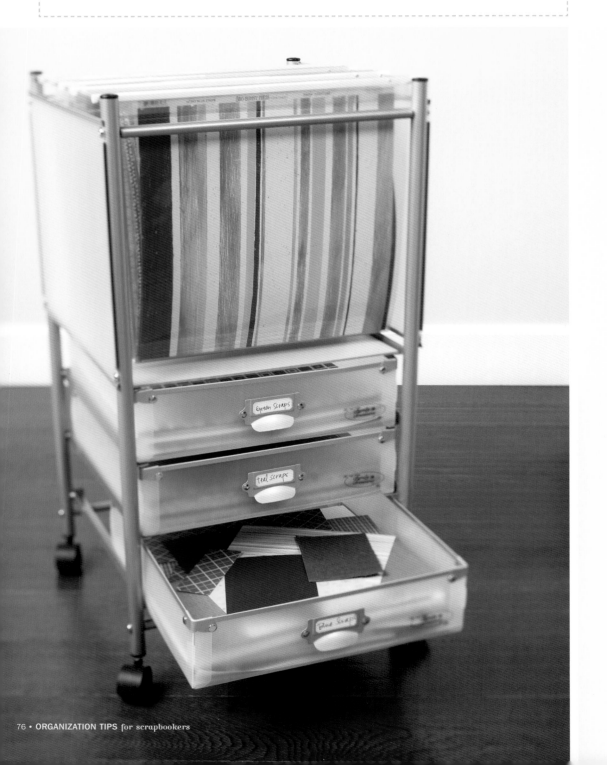

Scraps Under Wraps by BRITNEY MELLEN

Contain cardstock scraps in a portable color-coded file. A little stitching goes a long way to keep scraps from spilling out the sides.

WHAT TO GATHER:

- ☐ Expandable accordion file

- ☐ File folders (colored or manila—one for each color of scraps)

- ☐ Needle and thread

- ☐ Pen

- ☐ Sewing machine (optional)

Supplies *File folders and expandable accordion file:* Boon; *Pen:* Pigma Micron, Sakura; *Other:* Thread.

HOW-TO:

① Use a pen, stickers or rub-ons to label each file folder with a color that coordinates with the scraps you'll place in it.

② Stitch up the short sides of each file folder, leaving the top end open.

③ Divide cardstock scraps by color and store them in their respective file folders. Store folders in an expandable accordion file.

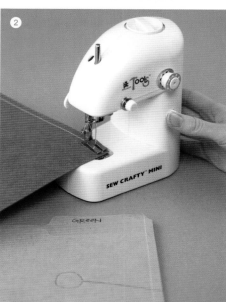

Travel Kit

Baby Kit

Kits

Store-bought, digital and subscription-based **page kits** are convenient, providing most **everything** you need to create coordinated albums, layouts and cards. **Explore** your options when it comes to **storing** them. You can find a method that keeps **materials together** as a coordinated set, or you can **split the products** up and mix them in with the rest of your **stash.** Your ideal storage **system** depends on **how you use** your kits.

READY TO GET ORGANIZED?

Gather the following:

- ☐ Album kits
- ☐ Calendar kits
- ☐ Digital kits (downloaded to a computer)
- ☐ Materials and photos gathered for upcoming pages
- ☐ Mini-book kits
- ☐ Monthly scrapbooking club kits
- ☐ Page kits

Sorting Purchased Kits

Some days, you may be on the fence about sitting down to scrapbook . . . and the thought of selecting photos and coordinating the materials for the page pushes you away. The beauty of purchased page kits is that most of the prep work is done for you—just add pictures and you're ready to play. If you discover sets piling up, however, it's time to organize so you don't forget what you've purchased.

Packets can be kept in their original packaging or removed and housed in document boxes or project files within bins, baskets or new white pizza boxes. Try classifying them by theme if you've already got photos in mind, by color if you'll be matching them up with photos later, or by project if you've earmarked kits for specific albums. (*For additional details on splitting up and indexing kit materials, see the Q&A on page 86.*)

Sorting Handmade Kits

If you love the kit idea but prefer to pick out your own materials, create the same sense of convenience by putting together a few do-it-yourself page kits. Simply choose photos for several layouts, then add the basic supplies to go with them whenever you have a spare minute.

Kits should include photos, cardstock and patterned paper, stickers, rub-ons or other accents, memorabilia, journaling notes, possible layout sketches and title ideas. Group materials for each page in the pockets of an accordion file, in the pouches of a vertical paper holder, or in page protectors inside an album or basket.

If you've compiled several kits, organize them by album or theme. Using tabs to note their subjects will help you find one to work on when the mood strikes. (Be sure to use removable labels or self-adhesive notes since the contents of the pockets will change constantly.)

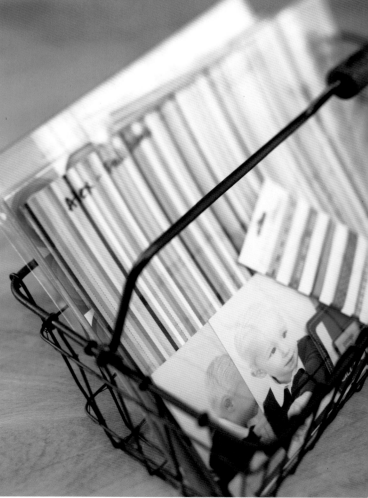

Organizing Digital Kits

What's the page-kit counterpart for digital scrapbookers? Digital kits, of course! Just like collections you can purchase to help coordinate and create paper layouts, digital kits contain supplies such as patterned papers, embellishments, alphabets and more. And just like a physical stash, you'll need a sorting system to help you organize and access the items you need. Create a "digital scrapbooking" folder on your computer and subfolders based on kits, online stores, digital designers or individual page elements.

Here's a quick tip: Digital scrapbooker Jessica Sprague drags all of the .jpeg kit previews into a main digital folder and uses the thumbnail view in Windows Explorer or Picasa to see all of the kits at once. After choosing the ones she's interested in and that coordinate with her layout's color scheme, she then goes into the subfolders for individual elements to incorporate onto her page.

Boogie Set

sunshiny kit

Q & A

Q: I subscribe to several kit clubs. Should I keep them together or store each element with the rest of my supplies?

A: If you always use the kit materials together to create coordinated pages and projects, keep them intact on shelves or in bins or drawers where you can grab the one that matches your photos. But if you buy them to try new products or to receive a sampling from different manufacturers, consider breaking them up, placing paper with your existing paper, new ribbon with existing ribbon and so on. You can always use sticky notes to jot a keyword, number or kit name on the patterned paper, cardstock and accents that belong together in case you need to group them again in the future.

Q&A

Q: My page kits are piling up. How can I remember which ones I have and where they're located?

A: Keep a running photo index to save yourself search time—when you receive a new kit, take a digital photo of the contents. Print it and write where it's stored on the back. (This can also help you identify which items belong together if you integrate kit elements with the rest of your stash.) Simply flip through the pictures when selecting materials for your next page—it's easier than flipping through kits piece by piece! Or keep a list on the front of each container, or start a section in your "idea file" to log the kit names, location, manufacturers, items, colors and themes they contain.

Expert Tips from LISA BEARNSON

"I store page kits in page pouches from Cropper Hopper, and several fit within one Vertical Paper Holder. Because they're clear, it's easy to see the photos and materials inside, so I can grab the page I'd like to work on. If the packets start stacking up, I'll label the paper holder as a quick reminder of what's inside the pouches."

Expert Tips from LEAH LaMONTAGNE

Without a place to organize her pages-in-progress, Leah LaMontagne says she'd forget what she needs to finish. She loves using a three-tiered paperwork organizer to keep everything in the open. Here's why:

■ The system is compact, but because it's tiered and made of clear plastic, all the elements are visible.

■ If she finds additional product that would be perfect for one of the pages, she knows exactly where to place it.

■ The pages don't get bent, lost or mixed up with other projects she's working on.

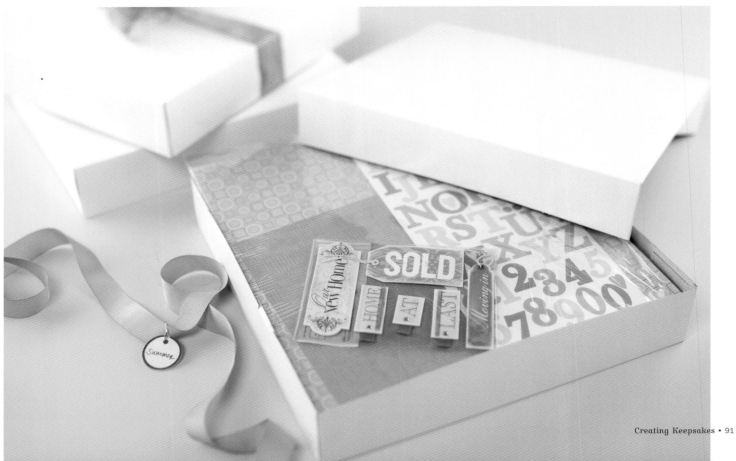

DOUBLE-DUTY STORAGE CONTAINERS

You don't always have to head to the store to find the perfect storage container. There are lots of places you can look for organizing solutions around your home—items that were purchased to organize one area of your home but that can be repurposed to use with your scrapbooking supplies. Consider the following possibilities:

- **TAKEOUT.** Use clean, empty pizza boxes for paper, condiment containers for tiny embellishments or salad cups for accents.

- **THE KITCHEN.** Use lid or dish-drying racks for cardstock, cup hooks for items that can be hung, bowls for stamps and inks, or cool mugs for pens and tools.

- **THE OFFICE.** Try letter-sized paper trays for cardstock, desk-drawer dividers for accents, and accordion files for everything from cardstock to stickers to scraps.

- **THE TRASH.** Well, before it becomes trash, that is. Reuse baby-food jars, drink carriers, glass bottles, boxes and gift bags.

Digital Directory by BRITNEY MELLEN

Every tech-savvy scrapbooker lives by the mantra "back it up!" when it comes to precious digital photographs. But have you thought about backing up your digital scrapbooking kits, too? Store several coordinating kits on one CD and include an index print with each disk for easy reference.

WHAT TO GATHER:

- ☐ Blank recordable CDs
- ☐ CD organizer
- ☐ Digital scrapbooking kits (locate the files on your computer)
- ☐ Empty CD cases

Supplies *Digital kits:* Winged Collection No. 1 and Audobon, Katie Pertiet, *www.designerdigitals.com*; *CD holder:* Target; *Other:* CDs and jewel cases.

HOW-TO:

① Save digital scrapbooking kits onto recordable CDs.

② Using your favorite photo-editing program, create an index print that shows the digital kit components included on each disk.

③ Slip index prints and disks into cases and store in a stacking CD organizer.

note cards

{CHAPTER 6}
cards

Cards

If your love of **paper-crafting** also finds you creating **handmade** cards,

you've probably got a stash of **blank cards** and envelopes in need of storage.

Establish an **arrangement** that lets you see and **sort all** of the available

colors and **styles** . . . and that will be a **good fit** for completed projects and

store-bought **greetings** as well.

Sorting by Level of Completion

If you're like most crafters, there are times you need to leave your studio mid-project, with raw materials, accents and tools sitting out in clusters and clumps. Because card basics are smaller than those for scrapbook layouts, they're more likely to be lost or forgotten amid the creative clutter. Instead of leaving these in-progress cards out in the open (especially where kids and pets can reach them), utilize a system that encourages you to file all of your projects and start them back up again without any hassle: store and sort cards based on the level of their completion.

An accordion file, for instance, can hold blank cards and envelopes, card kits, projects-in-progress and finished cards separately but in one convenient container. The same can be done with a binder, a drawer unit, a mini album, or a box, bin or basket with tabs dividing the sections. Or consider photo-display units for in-process storage.

Containers will also be a handy place to stow tags ready to affix to gifts and greeting cards that you couldn't resist purchasing. In-progress card storage will require the most organization, so you may want to pick a system for that first and then build your blank and finished card storage around it.

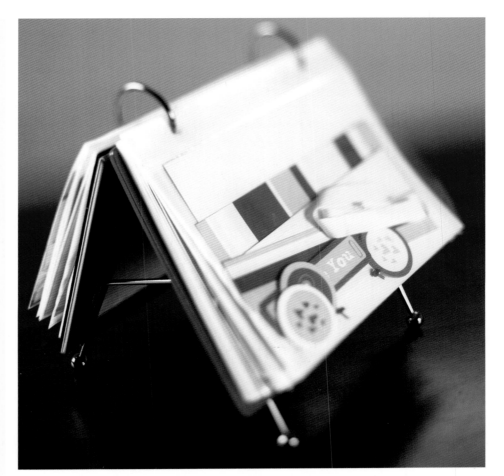

Sorting by Concept

You're a half-hour late for the party, stuffing a present into a gift bag and hoping you've got something about celebrations in your collection of finished cards and tags. Finding out if you do will only take a second if you've got everything stored according to concept. Devote sections of a small multi-pocket file, an entire tin or a space on a step-up, in-drawer spice rack to stow completed handmade and store-bought cards and gift tags. Divide projects into categories such as birthday, holiday, baby, wedding, sympathy, graduation, friendship and general celebrations. To remind you when you need to make a new card, place a reminder card at the back of each slot so you don't have to guess which category is missing once you've used your last card—this way, you'll always know which cards you need to restock.

Kits or materials you've gathered for future projects can also be filed in the unit according to theme for those times you want to create a card for a special occasion. You can also use leftover slots in the storage system to hold kits or supplies for similarly sized and themed mini albums.

Sorting by Format

One day you're in the mood to make a simple gift tag. On another, you endeavor to create a trifold card with overlays, swing doors and accents peeking through windows. Rather than rummage through an entire stack of blank cards for the proper card base to fit your mood, make finding the right one easy—separate cards according to their level of complexity or interactivity.

Divide blank cards by number of layers, foldouts, overall shape or the type and size of cutouts and windows. Designate a different section or drawer for each style, or keep them within reach in open storage, like a mail organizer, napkin holder, letter basket or divided photo box if you create cards as often as scrapbook pages. Ensure you've always got the correct, coordinated envelope by stashing them in one of two ways—with individual cards or arranged by size, shape or color in a nearby drawer or container.

GRAB-AND-GO OPTIONS

If you go to scrapbooking crops or card clubs frequently, you may want to store your cards in containers that can be transported quickly and easily. Storage units that are ready to go from tabletop to crop with no additional packing are great timesavers. Consider accordion files, portable bead caddies with removable boxes, plastic stacking jars or containers with secure-locking lids, poly envelopes with string ties, jewelry travel totes, zippered makeup bags, train cases, tool boxes with clamp closures, and zip-around pen pouches.

Q&A

Q: I've been creating more cards lately because layouts take too long. How can I find the time to make full-sized pages?

A: If you have organized supplies but no time to use them, you'll need to organize your time next. Take 20 minutes here and there to conquer small tasks. Then, when you do get an uninterrupted hour, most of the "prep work" for your pages will already be done. Try these ideas for your 20-minute breaks:

- ORGANIZE PHOTOS. Select images to use on your next layout.

- COORDINATE PAPERS. Choose a cardstock and patterned-paper combination.

- PICK ACCENTS. Find embellishments to support the theme.

- SKETCH. Come up with a few designs for the number of photos you plan to use.

- JOURNAL. Jot down notes about your photos or find an appropriate quote or lyric.

- BRAINSTORM. Flip through magazines to find design ideas, color combinations or title treatments to adapt for your pages.

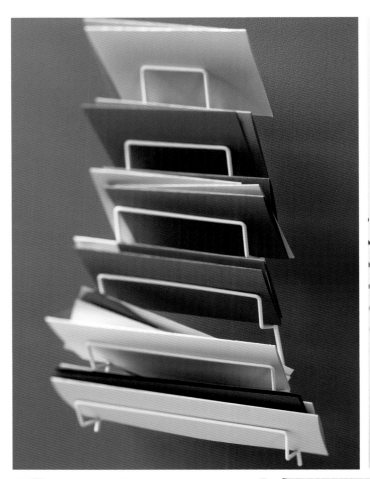

Expert Tips from JENNIFER McGUIRE

Because Jennifer McGuire makes cards almost as often as she makes scrapbook layouts, she needs to keep an ample stash of blank cards and envelopes on hand. Here's her method for storing them:

- Cards and envelopes sit in a large, deep drawer.

- Cards are unfolded and stacked together so she can instantly find the colors she needs.

- Envelopes are in the same drawer, sorted by size to allow her to grab the right one in a snap.

PLANNING FOR
THE YEAR AHEAD

If you keep a list of monthly birthdays and celebrations, consider storing your cards with the same concept in mind. Create a file folder or card keeper with 12 slots—one for every month of the year. Inside each folder, place a list of the cards you'll want to mail out. Then use your spare moments to make sure there's a card ready for each event on your list.

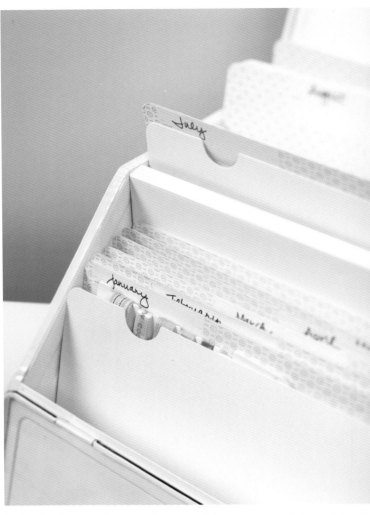

Card³ Catalog by BRITNEY MELLEN

Like to make beautiful handmade cards (or can't resist picking up those adorable greeting cards at your favorite card shop)? Wish you could easily locate the perfect sentiment for every occasion? Use a few simple supplies to create a card catalog and make sending the perfect card a breeze!

WHAT TO GATHER:

☐ 3-hole zipper pouch

☐ 3-ring binder

☐ Dividers with tabs

☐ Greeting cards and envelopes

☐ Page protectors for 4" x 6" photos

☐ Pens

☐ Postage stamps

☐ Return-address labels

Supplies *Binder:* Russell + Hazel; *Dividers:* Target; *Bookplate:* SEI; *Brads:* Making Memories; *Other:* Zipper pouch and page protectors.

HOW-TO:

① Sort greeting cards by occasion. Slip into page protectors.

② Label each divider with a category and place in binder. Add card-filled page protectors behind their respective dividers.

③ Fill a zipper pouch with pens, postage stamps, return-address labels and other mailing necessities. Place in binder.

Optional: Consider adding a section for addresses or a calendar to keep track of card-sending opportunities.

Creations

Ah, creating. Yep, it's **probably** one of my **favorite things** about scrapbooking. The **chance** to use my hands, to **play** with **paints** and **inks**—in short, to feel like **a kid again,** but in a more **sophisticated** way, of course [wink!]. There are **so many** techniques to try, so many ways to **experiment** and create one-of-a-kind **looks** on my pages, all with a **stash** of some **basic** tools of the **trade.**

And when the creative nudge comes, we all want to **sit down** and **scrap** before it has a **chance** to sneak away. The only way to **make** that happen, though, is to have **our spaces** in order so we can scrap **immediately,** knowing which inks are here and which tools are there. And once we **know where** "here and there" are—and **keep** all our supplies organized **accordingly**—we'll be able to sit down and **scrap** in no time!

{CHAPTER 7}
tools

Tools

As scrapbooking **grows** in popularity, so does the number of **tools** to make the **craft** more convenient. From **trimmers** to punches to paper **piercers**, there's an **apparatus** for every task—whether you **want** to make a shape, make a mark or just make an **impact.** If you find yourself scrambling for **necessities** whenever you design a page, **institute a system** to keep them better **organized** and completely accessible.

Sorting by Frequency of Use

Maybe you don't use your paper trimmer as much since you developed a knack for using a craft knife. Perhaps you turn to your templates more frequently now that you own a die-cutting machine. Not every tool in your arsenal will get equal time, so don't clutter your prime space with every tool you own.

Group tools by frequency of use and keep only your favorites close at hand. If you love to doodle, for example, let pens sit on your desk in a vase or pencil cup. If you don't use them much, stow them on a shelf or in a drawer. Or compile an "often-used tool caddy" to ensure the instruments you use to create every page will be at your fingertips.

And remember, your often-used supplies may not match those of your favorite scrapbooking buddies—that's okay! Group them in a multifunction tote, utensil caddy, drawer unit, tackle box or train case, or on a pegboard or a lazy Susan adorned with baskets, tins or paint cans that hold smaller items. (For suggestions on what to add to your "often-used tool caddy," see page 119.)

Sorting by Function

Want to improve the flow of your workspace? Sort tools by their primary function and compatibility. Keeping items that work together near each other means that you won't have to hunt for the hammer to hit the eyelet setter or the eraser to eliminate pencil lines. You may even want to store tools with their companion supplies (like a rub-on tool with the rub-ons) for extra convenience.

Make your decisions based on frequency of use and whether you use the tool for other functions as well. Since items will comprise a variety of sizes and shapes, try sorting by function in open boxes, bins or baskets to accommodate them all. Sample categories (and some of their basic tools) include:

- **Cutters** (trimmers, scissors, craft knives and rulers, decorative-edge scissors)

- **Dry embossers** (light box, stylus, brass templates)

- **Effects** (sandpaper, edge distresser, wire brush, paper crimper)

- **Fasteners** (anywhere hole punch, hammer, eyelet setter, self-healing mat, paper piercer, stapler)

- **Heat embossers** (heat gun, antistatic bag, tweezers)

- **Shapes** (die-cutting machines and dies, punches, alphabet and shape templates, texture plates, stencils, masks)

- **Writing utencils** (pencils, markers, pens, erasers)

Bonus Idea: If you use pens frequently and always find them rolling around on your desk when you scrapbook, find a small dish to keep them in place.

Sorting by Size

Whether you have a sizeable studio or a tiny scrap nook, space is always at a premium. Storing tools by size allows you to make the best use of containers and helps you remember where your tall, small and bulky gadgets are located in your area.

Organize narrow items like pens, eyelet setters and rub-on tools in cups, utensil caddies or narrow baskets and tins; scissors, hammers and handheld punches in wide-top baskets or hanging from a pegboard; punches in shallow drawers or pouches; templates in accordion folders or hanging-file baskets; and adhesives in a bucket or a rotating caddy.

If possible, give large equipment, such as personal die-cut machines, their own "station," where they can be used without being moved. Stow accompanying dies in shoe boxes, on a revolving rack or in binders on the shelf next to or beneath the machines.

Compacting supplies by size will not only make room for more, but it will also allow you to spend less time searching for what you need.

STOCKING YOUR TOOL CADDY

Trying to decide what you need in your tool caddy? Follow this simple trick: keep supply lists for the next five layouts you design, then compare what items consistently appear. Include those basics in your tool caddy. You'll typically notice a paper trimmer, scissors, adhesives and pens for your primary items. Consider making room for the following items as well:

■ **YOUR TRADEMARK TOUCHES.** If you often colorize with ink, create captions with alphabet stamps, or sprinkle flowers here and there, don't leave them out of your tool caddy.

■ **CURRENT FAVORITES.** If you like a particular style of fastener or prefer accents that require special tools, be sure to include them in your caddy.

■ **NEW PURCHASES OR OLDER PRODUCTS YOU MAY WANT TO USE.** Items staring you in the face are bound to find a place on your pages.

Expert Tips from LEAH LaMONTAGNE

"My tools fit perfectly in a repurposed spice organizer with the lids removed. The containers help me see what I need, and I can just pull tools out and drop them back in their places when I'm finished. It's not only a safe way to store sharp tools, but it's also cute and sophisticated at the same time!"

Q & A

Q: I tend to stockpile adhesives for fear of running out when I'm in the middle of a page. Where should I store the surplus?

A: Since you won't need the extra adhesives immediately, it's okay to stow extra adhesives—and other backup tools or supplies—in less-convenient storage. Stash them behind often-used items; in closed, flat bins beneath other containers (splurge on a few hip containers that can double as decor); or in an "extras" box in the closet where they'll be out of the way but still accessible. Just remember to keep your "supply inventory" list up to date so you don't end up buying more of what you already have.

Q & A

Q: My paper edges are jagged. My punches aren't making it through cardstock. My scissors are fraying my ribbon. Any solutions (other than buying new tools)?

A: Organized tools aren't useful tools if they're dull or gummed up with adhesive. Save time and money by taking good care of your tools *as you go*. Before you return trimmers, scissors and punches to their container, ensure they're ready for the next use with these maintenance tips:

- Change trimmer blades often to prevent ragged cuts through paper and photos (better yet, keep a few extras in your tool storage so you don't have to "finish this batch of cutting, albeit with ragged cuts" before you can make it to the store to purchase more).

- Keep punches and decorative-edge scissors sharp and smooth by periodically cutting through aluminum foil and wax paper.

- Remove residue from scissors and trimmers with Un-du adhesive remover. Be careful—it's also strong enough to wipe away ruler markings.

- Have straight-edge scissors sharpened professionally if they're not cutting crisply. Many craft stores offer this service.

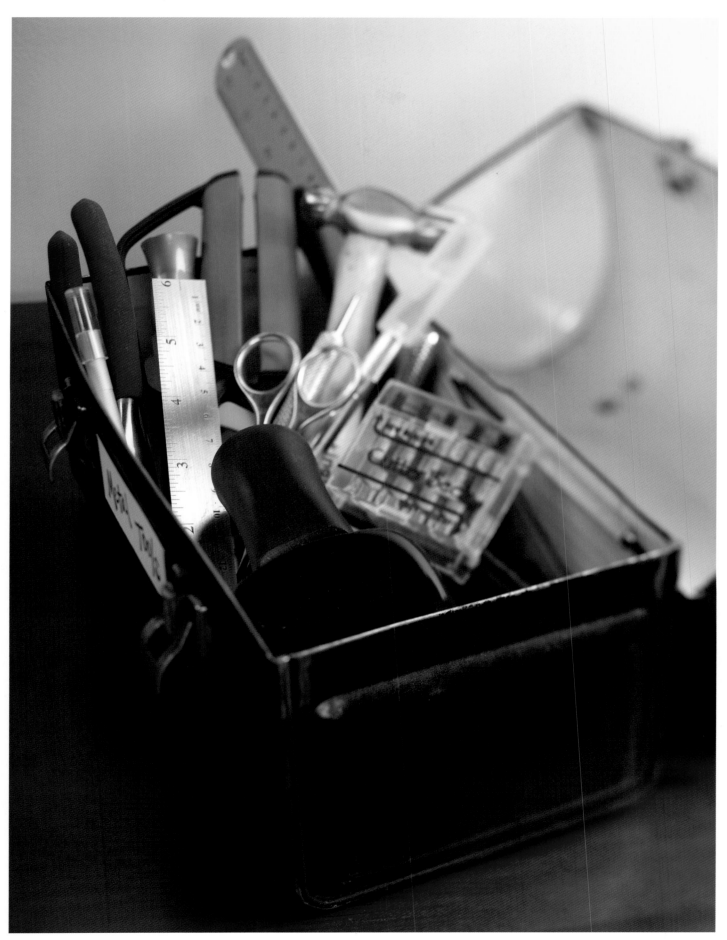

Expert Tips from BRENDA ARNALL

Brenda Arnall's work surface is an art table that gives her plenty of room to create. Her favorite feature? The attached tray holding the items she reaches for constantly. Here's why it works for her:

- The different-sized compartments hold pens, rulers, adhesives and cutting tools.

- She can grab everything quickly since it's all at her fingertips. It also takes no time to return items to the tray!

- The sections are deep enough to include accents, ribbon pieces and fasteners in small boxes or baggies.

Pockets Full of Tools by BRITNEY MELLEN

These easy-to-make hanging pockets keep tools within reach and off your work surface. Custom-size each compartment to give your favorite tools a snug (and attractive!) home.

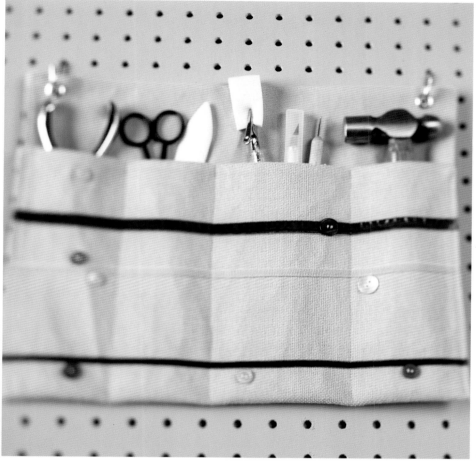

WHAT TO GATHER:

- ☐ Eyelets and eyelet setter
- ☐ Fabric placemat (embellished if desired)
- ☐ Hole punch
- ☐ Sewing machine (or needle and thread)

Supplies *Placemat:* Target; *Other:* Thread and eyelets.

HOW-TO:

① Fold placemat horizontally and lay tools on top, lightly making marks for stitching (pocket sizes will vary according to tool sizes).

② Stitch along marked lines to create pockets. Stitch both sides of placemat closed.

③ Punch holes along top of placemat for hanging and reinforce holes with eyelets.

Variation: Instead of hanging your tool holder on the wall, consider clipping it onto a skirt hanger for tool storage in a closet.

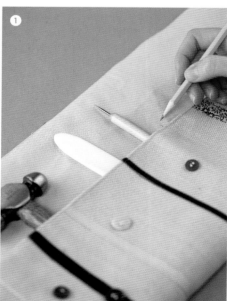

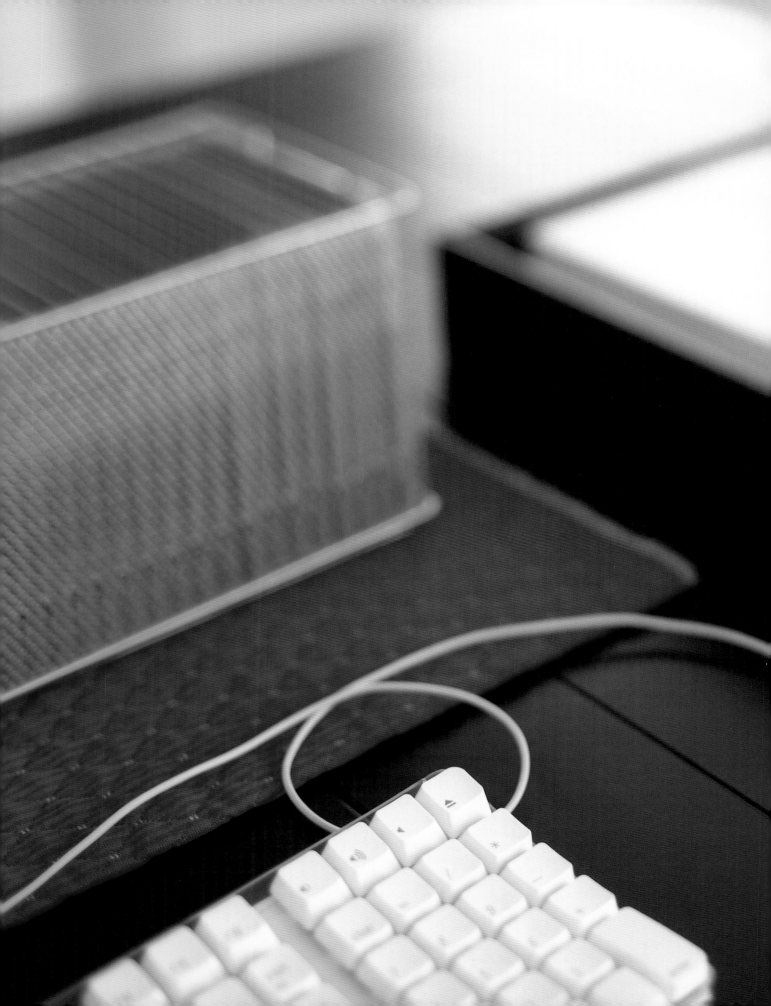

technology

Technology

Digital scrapbooking has opened up a world of creativity for **tech-savvy** scrapbookers, introducing new **concepts, techniques** and effects. But even if you're a **diehard paper** scrapper, technology still makes its way into your scraproom in the form of a digital **camera, scanner, computer** and printer. Let these **systems** help rather than hinder your workflow—**uncover** the best way to organize the **electronic elements** in your system.

READY TO GET ORGANIZED?
Gather the following:

- ☐ Backup CDs of files
- ☐ Cables and cords
- ☐ Camera equipment
- ☐ Computer
- ☐ Digital elements
- ☐ Digital files
- ☐ Font CDs
- ☐ Ink cartridges
- ☐ Manuals
- ☐ Printer
- ☐ Printer paper
- ☐ Scanner

Sorting by Convenience

When it comes to organizing your computer equipment and tech-related elements, more than just aesthetics comes into play. Design a "command center" based on convenience. Keep necessities—your computer, external hard drive, printer, scanner, card reader—and other fun extras within arm's reach and place related items next to one another.

Note how often you use each item and position them accordingly. For example, printers used frequently to output journaling or photos can be stored out in the open, while a scanner that's rarely used can be stowed on a shelf beneath your desk or in a cabinet.

When placing lesser-used items in cabinets, consider pullout shelving to make access easier when you do need them. Take extra precautions if you have small children— keep expensive, easily breakable or potentially dangerous items (and electrical cords) out of their reach.

Sorting by Supply

With technology comes paraphernalia . . . and lots of it. Printer paper, photo paper, compact discs, ink cartridges, manuals, chargers and cords, cords, cords—some of it you'll need now, but most of it you won't. Stash these technology-related items where they'll be accessible but compact. File photo and printer paper in magazine holders on your shelf, cords and cartridges in pockets of over-the-door accessory units, and software in a photo box or in page protectors within a spare mini album. *(For additional ideas on storing CDs of digital elements, fonts and photo backups, see the Q&A on page 137.)*

Storing in a Shared Space

If you share an office and computer equipment with your spouse, there's still a way to make it more creative for you while keeping it "professional" for him. If the walls, equipment, boxes and bins are a little too drab and industrial to feel inspirational to you, try a little altering if your significant other doesn't mind. Personalize with rub-ons or colorfully resurface file boxes and containers—not electronic equipment—with patterned paper, paint or stamped designs. If your husband won't appreciate that plan, hang a magnet board above the desk that you can decorate as a mini inspiration station. Decorate the walls with some of your favorite layouts and mini albums. Or place your "inspirational ideas" under the glass of your desktop.

Q&A

Q: My font, digital element and image-backup CDs are just lined up in a drawer. Is there a more creative way to store them?

A: Keep compact discs accessible and add a touch of decor to your room with wall-mounted CD ladders, cool shelving or over-the-door shelves. If you'd rather tuck them out of the way in your desk or on a shelf, try a revolving rack, CD wallet, pop-up organizer or cloth-covered CD album. Binders also make convenient storage—find storage sleeves with additional slots for index prints or blank cards for brief notes to describe what's on each CD.

SPACE-SAVING IDEAS

If you love the idea of computer equipment tucked away in cabinets and housed on pullout shelving, you'll find plenty of sources for similar space-saving designs. Kitchen stores are a good bet for innovative ways to stow supplies out of sight. Look for wire pantry organizers with sliding shelves, in-drawer spice steps, silverware caddies and two-tier lazy Susans to tuck items away. Or build upward, utilizing the space on your walls for all your tech-equipment needs.

Remember that you don't always need packaging for your gadgets either—if you can toss out the box (or store it with other boxes in an attic) and still recognize the contents inside, go for it to trim down your needed space.

Expert Tips from KELLY LAUTENBACH

"Since I share my studio with my husband's business, we've developed a 'make it work' system—and there are numerous extension cords involved in making it work! To conceal the mess and increase storage space, my printer sits on my desk atop a small cabinet big enough to hold surplus paper, inks and other supplies. Another benefit of the cabinet (and a larger bookshelf situated at the end of the desk) is that it serves as a 'screen' to keep visitors from seeing the jumble of cords!"

Q&³A

Q: I want to keep my tech supplies organized, but I already have my scrapbook storage in place. Is there any way I can integrate these supplies into my existing system?

A: More than likely, there is a great way! If you house supplies in document boxes, simply invest in a new box for your camera manuals and cables—and a second box, if needed, for your photo paper, ink cartridges, etc. If you store supplies in photo boxes, the same principle applies—but drop extra cables into smaller, enclosed 4" x 6" units before you place them inside. File folders, album storage and jars all work as well!

Expert Tips from C. D. MUCKOSKY

"One way I've organized³ the tech side of my scrap space is to deal with the wires—there were so many coming from different directions that I never knew what was leading where. Now I route all the cords through a hole at the back of the desk and plug them into surge protectors mounted beneath it. Cords are coiled in a wire basket suspended³ under the desk with small hardware hooks. It makes use of unused³ space, prevents tangles and keeps the floor cord-free."

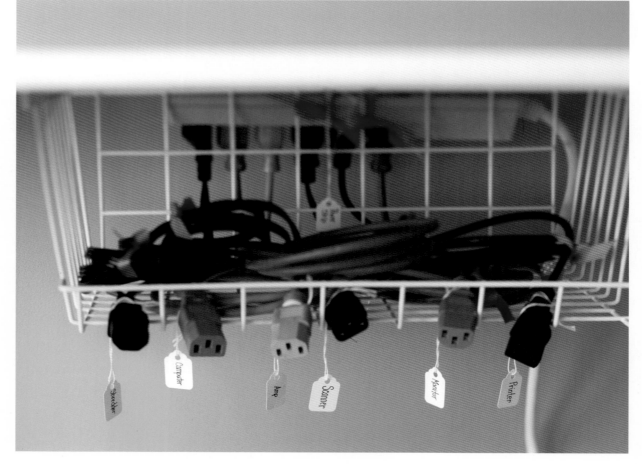

Keep Your Tech in Check by BRITNEY MELLEN

Your creative space is completely organized . . . except for the jumble of cords you encounter every time you connect your camera and photo printer. You aren't the only techno-gal to be pestered by cord chaos, but as a scrapbooker you do have an edge—the solution can be found right in your own stash of scrapbook supplies. Create a color-coded box to keep those cords in check.

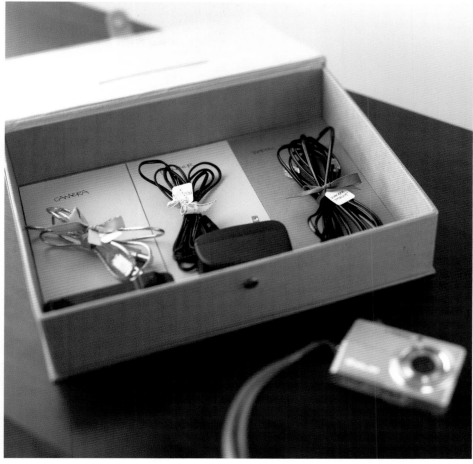

WHAT TO GATHER:

- ☐ Cardstock (trimmed to fit inside box)
- ☐ Cords, cables and chargers
- ☐ Document box
- ☐ Jewelry tags
- ☐ Pen
- ☐ Ribbon

Supplies *Document box:* Target; *Tags:* Avery; *Pen:* Pigma Micron, Sakura; *Other:* Cardstock and ribbon.

HOW-TO:

① Lay out all cords, cables and chargers and determine what device each belongs to. Assign a color to each type of cord, and tie a small tag to each cord using ribbon in the corresponding color.

② On small jewelry tags, write the name of the device for each cord, cable or charger; attach to ribbons.

③ Place color-coded cardstock strips in a document box to designate sections for each type of cord, then place cords in box.

{CHAPTER 9}

artistic materials

Artistic Materials

Paint, chalk, ink and other **colorants** have captured the **imagination** of **scrapbookers**, who love their versatility and their **ability** to generate numerous effects with **everything** from **altered** accents to **textured** backgrounds. If you've **discovered** the merits of artistic media, **select** a scheme to help you stock and **track** your **collection** of bottles, tubes, jars and **applicators**. Since a little goes a long way with these **products**, making sure you know **what** you have will **help** you keep from buying **duplicates** before you **need** them.

Gather the following:

- ☐ Acrylic paints
- ☐ Chalk applicators
- ☐ Chalks
- ☐ Cotton balls and swabs
- ☐ Decoupage pastes
- ☐ Dyes
- ☐ Embossing powders
- ☐ Fabric dyes
- ☐ Glazes
- ☐ Liquid adhesives
- ☐ Metallic rub-ons
- ☐ Modeling paste
- ☐ Paintbrushes
- ☐ Re-inker bottles
- ☐ Sponges
- ☐ Spray paints
- ☐ Stamping inks
- ☐ Texture pastes
- ☐ Walnut inks
- ☐ Watercolors

Sorting by Effect

Matte versus glossy is probably a consideration when you print photographs . . . but it can also be a decision to make when choosing a medium to work with. If you strive to achieve certain finishes on your projects, store jars, bottles and tubes according to effect.

Allocate space on your shelf or designate specific boxes to effects like texture, antique, matte, glossy, sheer, opaque, glitter and so on. Design a product "key" by applying samples of each medium on cards to let you see the entire collection at once—incredibly helpful if you want to select by effect and color, or if some products fall under multiple categories. While you're at it, save time by either dabbing a sample or noting the finish on the containers themselves so you won't have to double-check the fine print on each label.

Sorting by Type

Sometimes the most straightforward system is not only the most logical, but it's also the most convenient. Sort materials by type, such as paints, chalks, inks, metallic rub-ons, texture pastes, glazes, gels and dyes. It's a no-fuss method that will help you remember exactly what is where. Clustering this way can conserve space and time as well—you'll be able to house items you use most in containers like baskets, revolving racks and art caddies or on photo shelves above your desk, while lesser-used products can remain out of the way in airtight boxes or totes. If one of the groups grows by leaps and bounds, subdivide it into categories like color or manufacturer to make selection easier. You can even place favorite colors in your often-used tool caddy to reach them quickly.

Sorting by Level of Messiness

If you know you'll be creating your next page in the living room of a friend's home, you probably won't want to bring the paint along. If you can work creatively in a craft room or kitchen, though, messy paints won't be a problem. Keep similar items stored together by level of messiness, then you can simply grab one storage container and know you'll have plenty of materials to play with when you reach your creation station.

Sorting art materials by potential "oops" factor will also be helpful if you have small children—keep the most risky items stored up high or in cabinets. And think about creating a caddy specifically for junior crafters that includes washable markers, paints and leftover chalks they can use when working side by side with you.

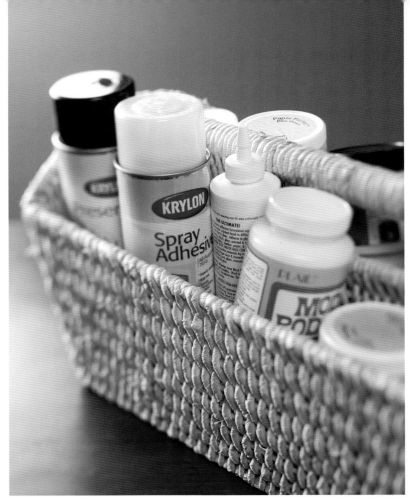

Q&A

Q: Cleaning and putting away paintbrushes is routine, but my other supplies are another matter. How can I keep my scrap space neat if "tidy" isn't in my nature?

A: Sometimes developing a "rule" will remind and motivate you to straighten. Experiment with one like:

- **BEFORE OR AFTER.** Return your space to order—filing scraps, returning products to containers, storing tools—before you create a page or right after you finish one.

- **TOSS TO TIDY.** To simplify cleanup, store supplies in bins and baskets. Open storage allows you to remove items and just throw them back when done.

- **LEAVE AN OUT.** Designate a "messy spot"—a box or bucket where you can throw scraps and unused items as you scrapbook. Periodically sort and file the items.

- **LET IT GO.** If scrapbooking amid the clutter fuels your creative process, there's no point trying to be excessively tidy. Just be sure to leave yourself a little room to work!

Expert Tips from LISA BEARNSON

"I store my paints in three Stamp Stacker Velcro storage pouches. Fourteen bottles fit in each pocket—and because they sit vertically (and compactly) on my shelf, I can quickly see and find the colors to match whatever project is at hand."

Expert Tips from JOY UZARRAGA

"I have a mishmash collection of paints in all sorts of bottles. I store them in a cleaning-supply caddy (you can find them in the cleaning section of Target, for example) so they're together in one place. I also keep my foam brushes and paintbrushes in a cup that slips into the caddy. The unit sits under my workspace, ready when I need it."

APPLICATOR STORAGE

The most popular "applicator" for colorants like chalks and rub-ons is probably an always-handy finger. But there are times when an actual paintbrush is a necessity. Keep your storage system intuitive by stashing applicators near their companion artistic materials so you can grab everything at once. Try hooking a pencil case onto your paint caddy, stuffing sponges into the drawer with inks, or housing painters' combs on the shelf with texture pastes. Or store applicators in a container near the sink or wherever you typically complete "messy" artistic techniques. If you use applicators for tasks such as brushing away eraser shavings, stow a spare in the container with your "dry" tools, like brass templates and craft knives.

Q &3 A

Q: My paints and art materials are lined up nicely on a shelf. Is there a way to avoid messing them up whenever I search for the proper shade?

A: What you see through the bottle or on the label isn't always what you'll get. Eliminate searches by dabbing the paint or finish onto the cap or a small tag attached to the bottle with ribbon or floss. You'll be able to see exactly what's in each container and mix and match at a glance. And if your bottles are nestled on a narrow shelf, run a line of double-stick tape along the surface—it'll tack the containers down so you won't knock everything off each time you remove or return one nearby.

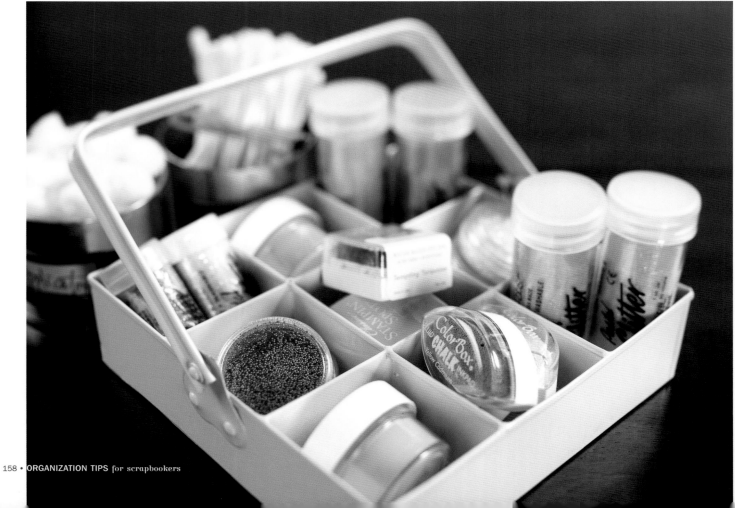

Artistic Effects by BRITNEY MELLEN

Don't play the guessing game when trying to figure out how a paint color will look on your scrapbook page once dry. Create 2" x 3½" swatch cards (the size of business cards) to keep track of different colors and effects achieved with your collection of inks, paints, chalks and other artistic materials. Store them in a small embellished binder that you can easily take with you when you go shopping for more supplies!

WHAT TO GATHER:

□ Black pen

□ Business-card organizer with 2" x 3½" transparent sleeves

□ Circle punch

□ Paint brushes, cotton swabs and applicators

□ Paints, inks, chalks, etc.

□ White cardstock

Supplies *Business-card holder:* OfficeMax; *Paint and eyelets:* Making Memories; *Pen:* Pigma Micron, Sakura; *Other:* Ribbon.

HOW-TO:

① Cut white cardstock into 2" x 3½" rectangles. Swipe, dab or brush a small sampling of paint, ink or chalk onto each card.

② Label each card with the color of the medium used. Once dry, insert cards into business-card binder sleeves.

③ Create tabbed sections for your binder by punching circles from the leftover white cardstock and labeling them with the correct title, such as paints, inks or chalks.

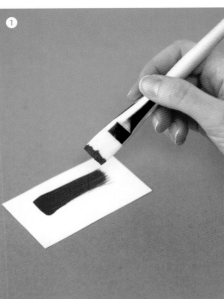

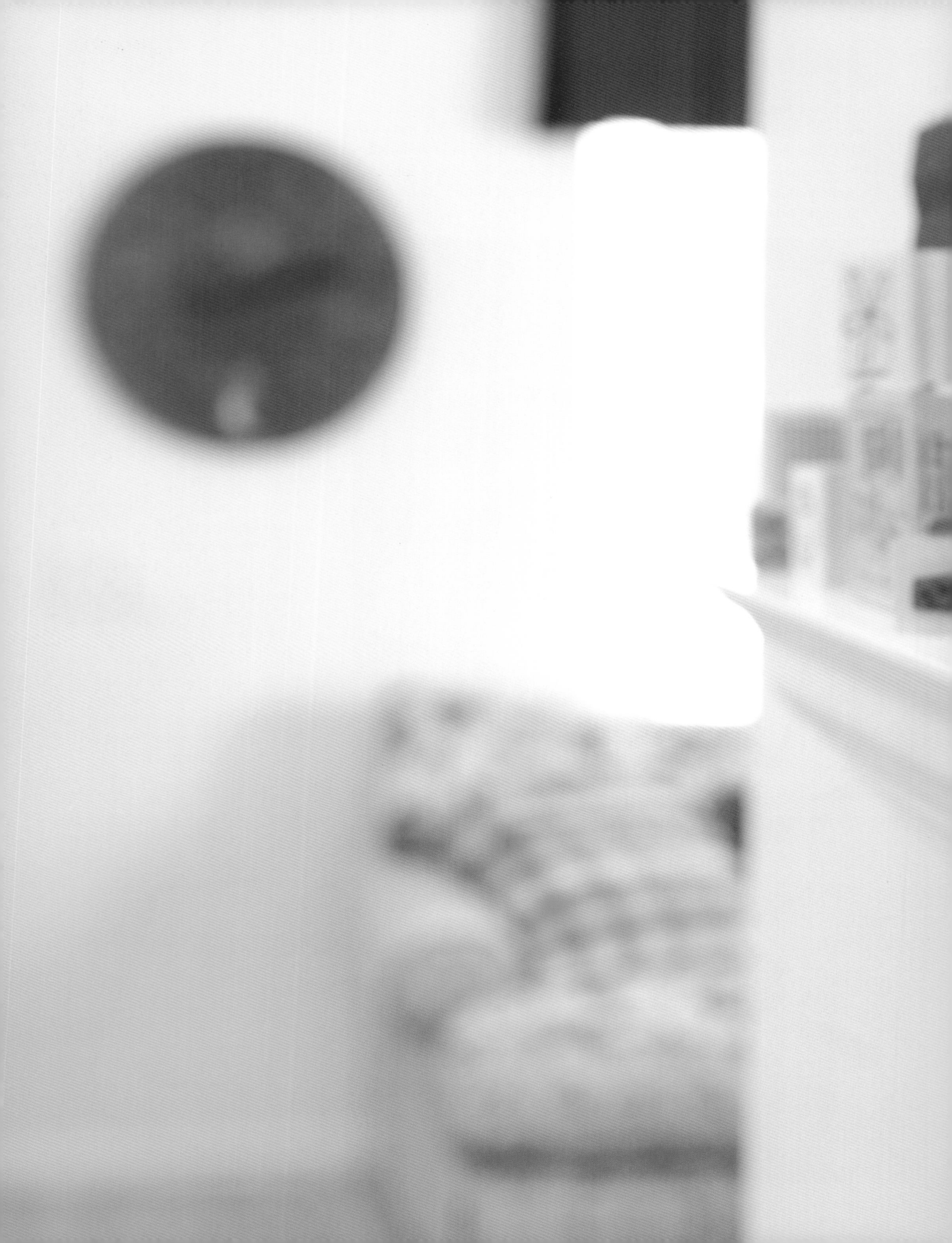

{CHAPTER 10}

stamps

Stamps

Stamps are **convenient**, are enjoyable to use and **generate** a lot of looks. Unfortunately, **wood-mounted** and **foam** varieties can also take up a lot of **space**, while unmounted versions can waste **a lot of time** if pieces are impossible to **identify**. Want to use **your** collection more? Pick a **compact storage** arrangement that helps you **remember the designs** you've got . . . and lets you **access** and **return** them easily.

READY TO GET ORGANIZED?

Gather the following:

- ☐ Foam stamps
- ☐ Unmounted rubber/acrylic stamps
- ☐ Wood-mounted rubber stamps

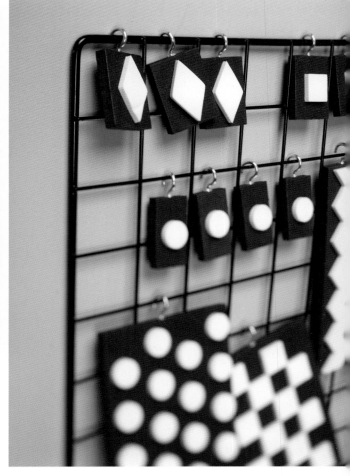

Sorting by Mounting System

While some crafters swear by unmounted stamps for their compact storage, others stick to wood-mounted because of convenience. You may have a combination of both—along with some foam stamps—if purchasing based on designs. Because of their size and method of use, however, a collection this diverse is probably best organized by mounting system.

Unmounted stamps will need to be stored in enclosed containers, like CD cases, binders or custom totes. Foam versions most likely belong in document boxes and storage cases or hung on magnet or pegboards. If washing foam stamps after use is always left forgotten, build a solution into your storage—consider a colander you can immediately take to the sink for washing; when the stamps are dry, return the colander to your scraproom.

Wood-mounted stamps provide several more options. Displaying them on spice-rack steps, photo shelves, wall-mounted racks and baskets will help you find designs in an instant (and provide some cool scraproom decor). On the other hand, tucking them into specialized cabinets, drawers or containers like acrylic frames, totes and shoeboxes will let you hold a lot more in a lot less space.

Although stamps may be separated by system, all of your stamps can be subdivided into the same categories, whether by size, theme or manufacturer, for quicker reference.

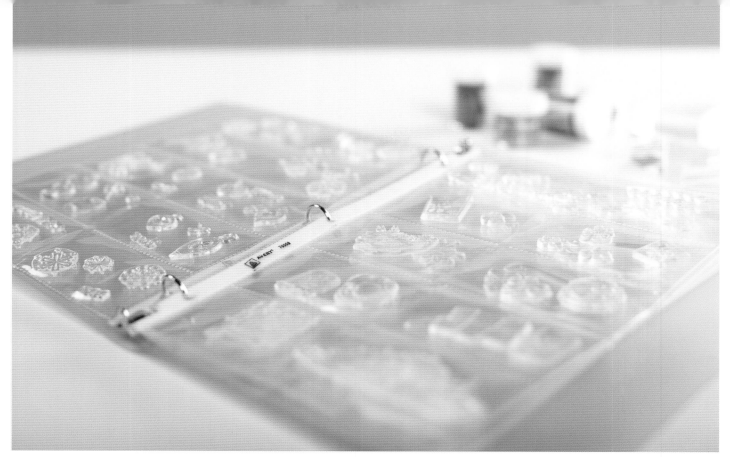

Sorting by Manufacturer

Stamping addicts can probably tell you which company created the stamp you're holding based on the style of the image. They may even know the designer of an alphabet stamp simply because of its size or font. If you're one of those savvy stampers who recognizes, purchases and uses a majority of designs from favorite product lines, then sort your stamps by manufacturer. Grouping by company will not only help you match designs and styles to the feel of your photos and layout, but it can also help you create coordinated cards with alphabets, sentiments and images that have a similar look and tone.

Once you're done sifting into whatever sorting and storage system you chose, create an index of images in your idea file or at the front of each container to see what stamps you have at a glance and to remember where they came from when it's time to clean up.

Sorting by Theme

Whether you're creating a greeting card, background, border or accent, you're definitely looking for a specific design to coordinate with your pictures or project. Sorting stamps by theme will help you find it. Consider organizing into the following categories—and sample subcategories if a group no longer fits into its box, drawer or tote:

- **Alphabets** (letters, numbers, punctuation)

- **Celebrations** (baby, graduation, birthday)

- **Design** (corners, flourishes, borders, journaling lines)

- **Holidays** (Valentine's Day, Easter, Fourth of July, Halloween, Thanksgiving, Christmas, Hanukkah, Kwanzaa)

- **Miscellaneous images and objects**

- **Nature** (flowers, leaves, animals, bugs)

- **Shapes** (circles, squares, hearts, stars, diamonds, rectangles)

- **Text** (words, greetings, backgrounds, dates)

- **Textures** (shadows, dots, lines, plaids, stitching)

If the "by theme" sorting system carries throughout your entire supply stash, you may want to attach sample stamped images near the coordinating categories of patterned paper and accents to remind you of the designs you have available in your stamp storage.

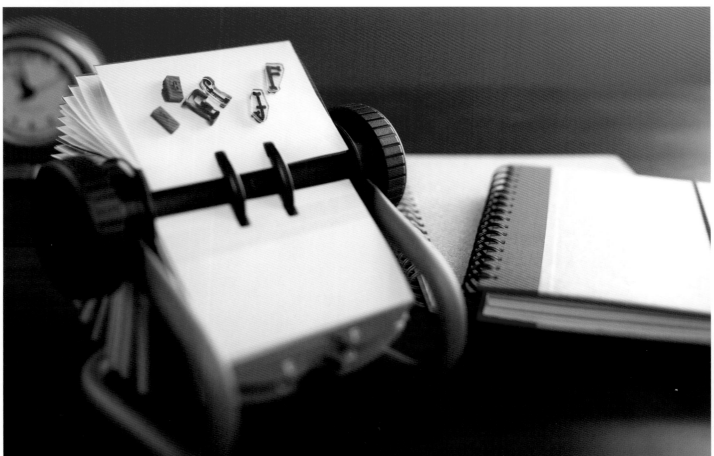

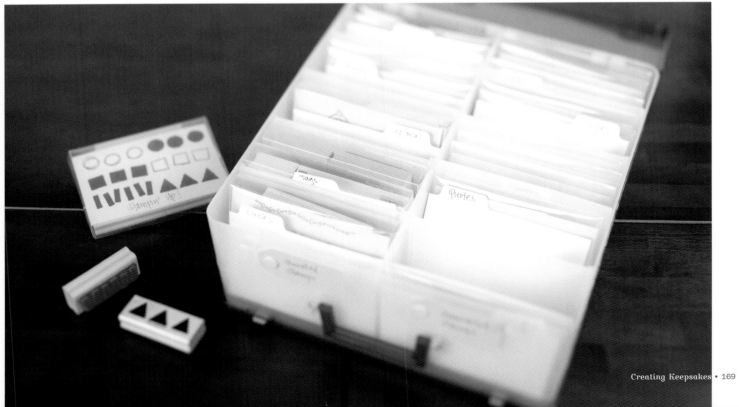

Expert Tips from ALI EDWARDS

Much of Ali Edwards' current storage system revolves around the idea that "like" items should be grouped together. Wood-mounted rubber stamps, for example, are housed in small metal tins, an organization idea that works for her because:

- Each tin holds stamps gathered into categories, such as lines, type, greetings, circles, favorites, dates and shapes.

- Open containers provide access and enough room to look for specific designs.

- The small buckets keep her stash size reasonable—she won't let herself acquire more than will fit in the bins, which means she continually evaluates which designs she gets to keep.

HARDWARE-STORE SOLUTIONS

Home-improvement warehouses are a goldmine of organization finds. Wander the aisles in search of items like tilt bins for ribbon and accents; plastic tool boxes for paints, stamps and inks; nut and bolt containers with multiple drawers for embellishments; utility trays for pens, applicators and tools; rain gutters for ribbon spools; or metal sheets to create do-it-yourself magnet boards. If the items are too industrial for your taste, personalize with rub-ons, stamps, paint, ribbon, stickers and more.

Q & A

Q: Keeping my stamps on open shelving helps me instantly see the design I need. How can I locate supplies that aren't stored out in the open just as easily?

A: Your scrapbooking time is valuable—organize to help yourself pinpoint and reach materials quickly. Here are a few ways to find anything fast:

- **GET IN THE ZONE.** Store items in zones that reflect the order and manner in which you select page materials to make finding the right supply intuitive (consider the four main sections in this book).

- **SPREAD OUT.** Rather than store boxes upon boxes, follow the "two-layer rule" wherever possible—try not to stack storage items or trays more than two layers deep in any drawer or container. They'll be easier to access, which means you're more likely to use them.

- **MAKE IT CLEAR.** Clear plastic boxes, bins or bags can help you identify items immediately.

- **LABEL.** Although you think you'll remember where everything is stashed, make sure you do—by tagging every container, whether by general category or with an in-depth list of all items inside.

- **PARE DOWN.** Are you spending more time looking for product than actually using it? Maybe it's time to slim your stash. *(See the Q&A on page 208 for tips on purging your unused supplies.)*

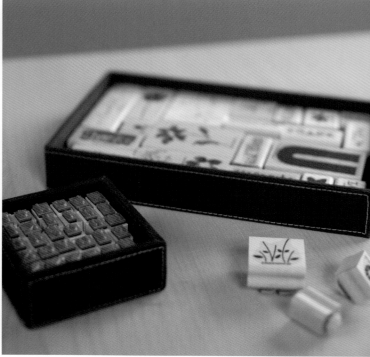

Expert Tips from BECKY HIGGINS

"Although some of my foam stamps came in packaging that's fine for storage, the majority of my sets are in Cropper Hopper 12" x 12" Paper Organizers. With a 12" x 12" piece of foam core slipped inside to help fill the space a little bit, the stamps sit flat inside instead of piled into a box or plastic bag. I simply open the flaps on the organizer to grab the designs I need."

Q&A

Q: Should I keep stamp sets together or mix them in with others of similar shapes and sizes?

A: Sets are compiled to create an overall "look," with coordinated designs or themed collections designed to go together. Keep them intact if you like images on projects to have the same feel or if you're already grouping by manufacturer, since sets will fall into the same category anyway. If you typically use stamps individually, break sets up and stash pieces within your themed categories. But before you do, label each stamp's side with the set name and manufacturer in case you ever decide to reunite the sets.

Stacks of Stamps by BRITNEY MELLEN

Pizza boxes are an unlikely candidate for stylish storage, but their size and depth lend themselves perfectly to storing your stamp collection. Slip a stamped reference sheet into the bottom of each one and stamp out disarray forever!

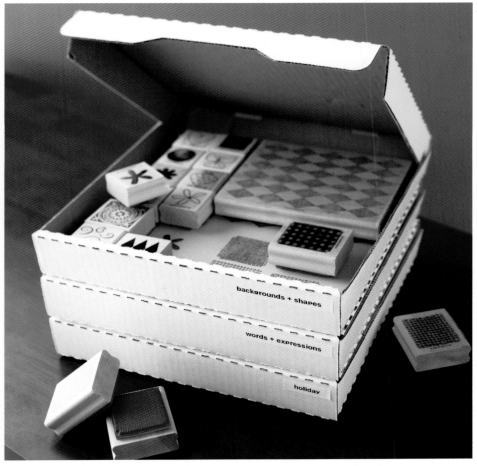

WHAT TO GATHER:

☐ Black ink

☐ Cardstock

☐ Labels, pen, stickers or rub-ons for labeling

☐ Pizza boxes (one for each category of stamps)

☐ Stamp collection

Supplies *Cardstock:* Bazzill Basics Paper; *Stamping ink:* Stampin' Up!; *Label tape:* Dymo; *Pizza boxes:* Papermart.com.

HOW-TO:

① Sort stamps into categories.

② Trim cardstock to fit inside the pizza boxes and use black ink to stamp each image onto cardstock. Be sure to space images so the stamps will fit properly on top of the corresponding images.

③ Place a stamped sheet in the bottom of each box. Place each stamp over the stamped image. Label each box by category. Even if you take out several stamps at a time, you'll always know right where they belong, so cleanup will be quick and easy!

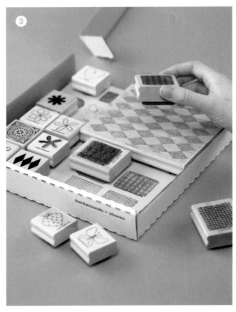

Decorations

They're the icing on the cake—the **brads**, **buttons**, **letters**, **ribbons**, **rub-ons**, **stickers** and more that can help us transform our pages from **sweet** to sensational. They're also **generally small** enough that they can get **lost** and forgotten in a collection of unorganized supplies. And **remember**, out of **sight** can mean out of **mind**—and thus out of your scrapbook. But there is a way to **sort and store** these "decorations" in a way that's **usable** for you. And it all **depends** on how you use these **amazing** embellishments.

Whichever **systems** on the following pages are **right** for you, you'll love how they **allow** you to find what you need when you **want it**, helping you create your **treasured** scrapbook pages in **no time!**

{CHAPTER 11}

letter accents

Letter Accents

Hand-lettering, stamping and **using fonts** will always be **popular** ways to **create titles** and **journaling**. On the other hand, nothing adds texture and makes things pop like **dimensional** number and alphabet **accents**. **Deciding** which ones to use on your next page **may be difficult**, but with these ideas, **coming up** with the **ideal** storage for them doesn't need to be! If you're favoring chipboard, metal, acrylic or fabric **letters** lately, stash them in a **manner** that allows you to **sift through** them to find the right **letters** for the right **words**.

Sorting by Individual Letters

If you keep each set of dimensional alphabets in its own container or compartment, there's always the one time you rummage through (and rummage through again) only to find that you're one "e" short of a complete title. How can you instantly detect all of the "e's" you have left and make mixing and matching or selecting monogram accents a breeze? Just throw caution to the wind—combine all of your alphabet sets into one big pile, then sort them by letter instead of by font. Many bead boxes feature enough compartments to hold individual letters, groups of numbers and punctuation.

If your collection is extensive or includes large chipboard or acetate letters, try a custom organizer or gather groups in votive holders or tins lining shallow drawers or baskets. Attach a sample letter to each or stamp letters onto the containers with solvent ink as cute labels that will help you quickly find the letters you need.

Sorting by Typography

Do you ever use a computer to design and output journaling? Unless you use the default Times New Roman font for all your text, you've probably developed a method for selecting a font for your layouts. Divide your physical alphabet collection along the same lines so you can pick lettering to support the mood and theme of your page.

Whether they're chipboard, fabric or acrylic, the letters will either be serif or sans serif and may fit into such categories as script, typewriter, calligraphy, outline, stencil, western or graffiti. If you'd rather separate by the overall look and style of the figures, try groupings like cute, classic, funky, formal, modern, retro or grunge.

Consider designating a jar, tin or basket for each style, then keep individual sets grouped inside. For consistency, classify your letter-stamp systems into the same categories. If your letter storage space is large enough, you could even store your letter stamps within it!

Sorting by Material

As you envision your layout, you probably spend as much time visualizing the look of your lettering as you do deciding what you want to say—a look that can be heavily influenced by the letters' material. Simplify the selection process by allocating a box, drawer or bin to each of the following material categories: acrylic, fabric, metal, plastic, chipboard and acetate. When you need charming letters to lend a textured and homey touch to a page, head to the "fabric" drawer. When you want a title you can sand and distress, try the chipboard bin. Since the categories are fairly broad, you'll need to develop a way to subdivide them—such as by color, manufacturer or font—unless you want to plow through an entire container to find one letter.

PACKAGING—TO STOW OR LET GO

As scrapboookers, we love packaging—especially when it's almost as hip as the product inside. So how do you know when to keep it and when to toss it? Try these ideas:

- **SMALL LETTERS.** You may want to keep the packaging for small letters. They can easily become lost outside of packaging if you store them loose in a large bin.

- **LARGE LETTERS.** You should be fine parting with the packaging for bulky letters. They not only require larger boxes to store, but they probably won't get lost as easily when you shuffle your supplies.

- **MULTICOLORED LETTERS.** You might want to toss your packaging for multicolored sets, especially if you always use monochromatic color schemes on your pages. You can sort the letters by individual color outside their original packaging.

- **LETTERS HIDDEN INSIDE AN OPAQUE BOX.** Consider tossing opaque packaging so you can see the letters in plain view. If "out of sight, out of mind" sounds familiar to you, then only keep packaging with clear windows that reveal the contents inside.

Q&A

Q: What should I do with the "unpopular" letters that I never seem to use?

A: Letter stickers are easy to cut apart and reassemble into new figures—turning an "h" into an "l," "n," "u," "r" or "i," for example. Dimensional letters are more of a challenge, but chipboard, acetate and fabric versions can still be snipped apart. Button-style letters can be altered with solvent ink. Your best bet for leftover engraved metal tiles is flipping them over and adding sticker or stamped letters to the back.

If you have more than a handful of remnants, organize a swap with friends—they may be searching for letters that are just sitting in your stash. Or, use them as monograms. You can also add them to journaling blocks on playful pages to give your text a new look.

Expert Tips from LAURIE STAMAS

Rub-ons in "books" are convenient, packing a lot of letters into a little space. But unlike designs on full, flat sheets, these don't slip as readily into files or folders. Laurie Stamas found the following solution: storing packs in sleek metal tins. Here's why it works for her:

- She places a piece of the original plastic packaging in the middle of the tin, dividing it in half. White rub-ons are stored on one side, black on the other, with colors in the back of each row.

- With the font size and color facing out, she can quickly thumb through the packs to find the design she wants for a specific page.

- The inexpensive system is compact enough to sit next to her workspace—a plus since Laurie uses rub-ons often.

Expert Tips from DENISE PAULEY

"While I keep my sheets of dimensional alphabets with similar materials (chipboard letters in the chipboard drawer, fabric with fabric and so on), I store acrylic, metal and button letters according to letter. Carousel Craft Organizers keep everything visible and accessible with a quick spin. Though you can stack several (each one has 12 removable containers), I just use two and double up the "less popular" letters to make room for numbers and punctuation. As a bonus, the open center is convenient for holding the specialty adhesives I sometimes use to adhere them."

Q&³A

Q: I'd like to group by type, but some of my letters are loose while others are part of larger sheets. How can I combine them into one storage system?

A: Breaking sheets apart isn't always a possibility, especially if the letters are self-adhesive. (You may have similar problems with fabric tabs, paper die cuts and chipboard.) Develop a system that keeps everything together inside one of these units:

- DRAWERS—Store sheets along the side and loose pieces in smaller bins inside.

- BINDERS—Place sheets in page protectors and tuck loose pieces in binder sheets with smaller, resealable pockets.

- MULTI-POCKET FILES—Slip sheets into the accordion file in back and utilize the pockets for loose letters.

- DOUBLE-SIDED BOXES—House loose items in the compartments on one side and sheets in the deeper section on the other.

Keeping Tabs by BRITNEY MELLEN

Your Blackberry may be the best way to keep track of family and friends, but don't throw out that old address book! It's a fantastic place to store your letters. Just attach envelopes to the inside pages and you'll be keeping tabs on your letter stash in no time. A small address book works great for all the "leftover" letters. If you're planning to store every full set of letters you own, you may want to go for a larger address book instead.

WHAT TO GATHER:

- ☐ 26 envelopes (one for each letter of the alphabet)

- ☐ Address book (with alphabet tabs and pages large enough to accommodate your choice of envelopes)

- ☐ Adhesive

- ☐ Letter stash (fabric, chipboard, metal, plastic and so on)

Supplies *Address book and envelopes:* Paper Source.

HOW-TO:

① Sort letters into piles (one for each letter).

② Adhere an envelope to each page of the address book.

③ Place letters in corresponding envelopes.

flat embellishments

Flat Embellishments

Although they're **low profile**, flat accents like stickers, rub-ons, die cuts and punch-outs can be **high-impact** on your layouts. The relatively **compact** embellishments still need roomy, **sturdy storage** that prevents pieces from **buckling**, getting lost or sticking to one another and that permits easy rummaging when you're **conducting** a search.

READY TO GET ORGANIZED?

Gather the following:

- ☐ Die cuts
- ☐ Ephemera (store-bought for embellishments)
- ☐ File folders and envelopes
- ☐ Journaling cards
- ☐ Preprinted punch-outs
- ☐ Rub-on sheets
- ☐ Stickers
- ☐ Tags

Sorting by Size

Despite the fact that all of your flat embellishments have the same dimension (or near lack thereof), their lengths and widths can run the gamut from a tiny jeweler's tag to a 12" x 12" sheet of rub-ons. Organizing by size can conserve space and keep smaller items from getting lost or damaged in the shuffle. If you've got the room, consider buying one accordion file or basket for each size of sticker or rub-on sheet. Use file tabs to divide those by type of embellishment, manufacturer, color or theme.

Sheets can be housed in or out of their original packaging, but if you do unpack rub-ons, here's a tip: immediately staple the rub-on sheet to the backing sheet to prevent designs from sticking where they don't belong.

If you'd rather combine everything into a single drawer unit or hanging file, group smaller items in envelopes to find them easily. Smaller accents like die cuts, tags and ephemera can be similarly stored in an index-card file or photo box.

Sorting by Design Element

Back in the day, flat embellishments were pretty much limited to stickers and die cuts. These days, there are sticker, rub-on, punch-out and cardstock products that can be used for every aspect of your layout. Separate your stash by page elements, including the following categories:

- **Accents** (die cuts, punch-out shapes, image stickers and rub-ons, ephemera, file tabs, tags)

- **Borders** (border stickers, paper ribbon, die cuts)

- **Journaling** (tags, preprinted journaling spots, mini envelopes and file folders, sticker bookplates, library pockets)

- **Photo mats** (cardstock frames, transparency overlays, photo corners)

- **Titles** (alphabets, quote and word stickers/rub-ons, frames, tags)

With this system, if you're designing a photo mat, for example, head to the container filled with mat-related materials. If something can be used in more than one category, such as tags, place a few in each file or include a note where they're located.

Sorting by Season

Here's a little spin on organizing stickers, rub-ons and preprinted accents by theme—one that's particularly helpful if your container doesn't have many compartments or if your stash isn't that extensive. File by season. Most themed accents can fall under winter, spring, summer or fall. Even "generic" shapes evoke the feel of certain seasons, like hearts for winter (Valentine's Day) or stars for summer (Fourth of July). But if you've got several that fit into more than one (baby or birthday) or don't fit into any (plain circles or squares), create a fifth folder for miscellaneous images. Add an index to each folder or section to remind you of the contents. Sample themes for each season include:

- **Winter** (Christmas, Hanukkah, Kwanzaa, New Year's Eve, Valentine's Day, hearts, snow, winter sports)

- **Spring** (Easter, flowers, nature, wedding, spring sports)

- **Summer** (Fourth of July, beach, picnic, vacation, stars, summer sports)

- **Fall** (Halloween, Thanksgiving, school, leaves, fall sports)

Expert Tips from JOY UZARRAGA

"I store my stickers and rub-ons in document boxes organized by manufacturer. I chose this system because most sheets have multiple colors, which would make it more difficult to find what I'm looking for if I sorted by color. Also, some manufacturers have styles I can match to the mood of my page. For example, if I'm looking for something whimsical, I sift through my KI Memories or Doodlebug Design stash."

Q&A

Q: If I'm sorting stickers and rub-ons by color or theme, where do I store sheets that feature multiple colors or designs?

A: If storing by color, an easy solution is to create a new "multicolor" category for your files. If you'd rather not, identify the main color on the sheets or decide which color you'd most likely use them with. If sorting by theme, file according to the predominant subject or by the sticker on the sheet that led you to purchase it.

If you have several stickers that don't fit into any category, your themes may be too specific. Try broadening a little—instead of individual holidays, birthdays and events, for example, simply group them all under "celebrations" instead.

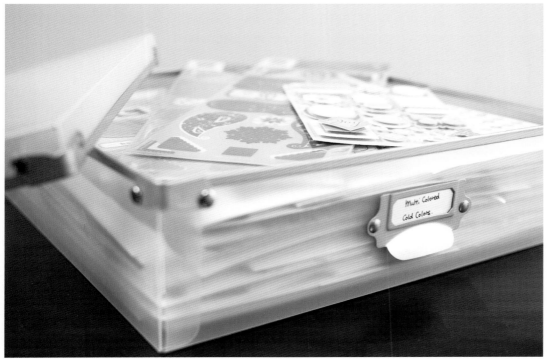

Q&A

Q: Should I store letter stickers with my other flat accents or with my dimensional letter accents?

A: When you create a title for your layout, what's the first element you consider—the color? size? texture? If any type of letter will do and if you frequently mix and match flat and dimensional pieces, then create a "letter station"—a drawer unit or file box housing all of your alphabet and number accents. But if you choose pieces based on their look (chipboard, fuzzy, epoxy, acetate), it will be more convenient and space-friendly to keep the dimensional accents together and the sticker sheets with other flat embellishments.

Expert Tips from BECKY HIGGINS

"I keep my stickers and rub-ons in a variety of Cropper Hopper Expo files. The accordion folders come in several sizes, such as 5" x 7", 7" x 12" and 12" x 12", and they are perfect for categorizing by type or manufacturer. I can add labels to the outside as well as to the interior tabs for easy access to any style I'm looking for."

Q & A

Q: I can't possibly use all of the supplies I've got, but how can I decide what to cut from my stash?

A: Sometimes it's tough to part with supplies you love (or once loved). But when boxes and drawers overflow and you're spending a majority of your scrapping session searching for materials, it's time to sift. How can you decide what to let go? Ask yourself the following questions:

- Is it more than two years old? The old clothing rule applies here, too—if you haven't used it by now, you probably never will.

- Can I think of an immediate use? Confess—did you buy it just because it was "cute"? Don't keep it if you can't actually see yourself using it.

- Has my style changed? Though you liked something once, if you won't let it grace your pages now, there's no point holding onto it.

- Can't decide? Put the item in a bin away from your space. If you've created several layouts without noticing its absence, it may be easier to part with.

Sticker Spinner by BRITNEY MELLEN

Are your file folders or storage drawers overflowing with stickers and rub-ons? Wish you could easily find your flat embellishments in just one spin? Here's an easy desktop solution using sheet protectors, binder rings and a vertical paper towel holder.

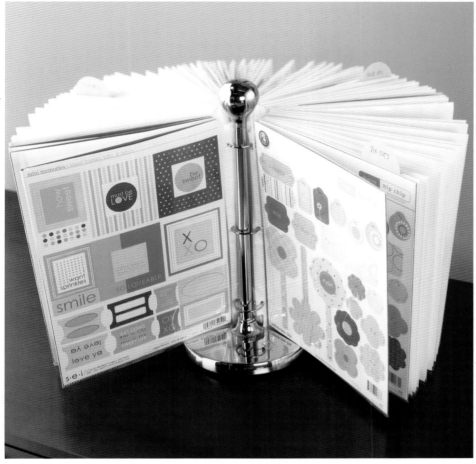

WHAT TO GATHER:

- ☐ 3 1½" binder rings
- ☐ 100 8½" x 11" sheet protectors
- ☐ 100 8½" x 11" sheets of white cardstock
- ☐ Flat embellishments
- ☐ Vertical paper-towel holder

Supplies *Paper-towel holder:* Umbra; *Other:* Page protectors and binder rings.

HOW-TO:

① Slip a piece of sturdy cardstock into each sheet protector for added stability.

② Slide your embellishments into sheet protectors.

Note: Depending on the number of embellishments you own, you may have empty sheet protectors for now. But that's okay—it's much easier to assemble the spinner now and add new embellishments in the future.

③ Attach page protectors together with three binder rings. Slip binder rings onto a vertical paper-towel holder.

dimensional embellishments

Dimensional Embellishments

Dimensional **accents** are a quick way to add "a little something" to your layouts. Make using them **even easier** with a system that **helps** you keep track of **everything** from tiny eyelets and **delicate** flowers to jumbo chipboard shapes and heavy metallic frames. Choose a **method** that will help you **instantly locate** the perfect piece to **coordinate** with the color, mood or theme of your **page**.

Sorting by Packaging

Packaging or no packaging? That is the question. Removing accents and other products from original packaging can save you lots of space in your scraproom, letting you consolidate items within smaller containers to make searching simple. Perhaps you want to keep everything intact until you use it, though, so you can remember manufacturer and product details. Or maybe you want to keep layout samples handy or make sure small pieces in a set don't become lost or misplaced.

When storing items in packaging, find creative ways to hold and sort them at the same time. Try a large pegboard to display groups of accents in clamshell packaging. Hang pouches of beads from clips on magnet boards. Dangle packs of chipboard sheets from a dowel, rod or cup hooks. Or cluster items by manufacturer in canvas bins, by type in large buckets, or by theme in locker baskets or drawer units. (If you do decide to discard packaging, see page 222 for tips on remembering product details.)

Sorting by Function

Accents may be the most decorative part of any page, but they can definitely serve other purposes as well. Classifying embellishments by function allows you to grab the right container whether you want to attach, or adorn, flag or frame. Bead and floss boxes, watchmaker tins and spice jars are ideal for separating tiny items like beads and fasteners, while larger items like bookplates and chipboard shapes are well suited to tilt bins, drawer units and candy jars. Bulky and odd-sized pieces—and those still in original packaging—can be conveniently contained in baskets, photo boxes and canisters.

Once divided, think about placing the containers near others with similar contents—fasteners close to tools, flashy accents by glitter and glitzy media, purely decorative embellishments beside stickers and so forth. Sort into function-related groups like:

- **Decorations** (charms, tiles, flowers, coasters, chipboard shapes, dimensional stickers)

- **Fasteners** (eyelets, brads, conchos, pins, paper and metal clips, photo turns)

- **Frames** (frames, bookplates, photo corners)

- **Glitz** (beads, sequins, gems)

- **Text** (metal words, word beads, printed labels)

Sorting by Shape

Looking for an accent to adorn your page? If you're like most scrapbookers, you're probably searching for one based on its shape. So, sort that way, too! Separate your items into basic categories like flowers, circles, squares, rectangles, ovals and stars. If your container has multiple compartments, subdivide by color or theme. Small groups can be stored in stacking canisters, resealable pouches in a binder or even in a row of cool glasses on a shelf.

But if you're willing to loosen up a little on the sorting, you can actually save storage space by using a few large containers rather than several smaller ones, especially if narrow categories keep those containers only partially full. Who knows, when sifting through an entire photo box of flowers (instead of smaller units of paper flowers, silk flowers and chipboard flowers stored individually), you may find a style of embellishment that will look even better than the one you'd planned.

Bonus Idea: When storing items like beads that are often poured onto liquid adhesive, consider a container with a spout for easy pouring.

Expert Tips from REBECCA SOWER

Fabric, buttons and notions add character and charm to Rebecca Sower's layouts. In her scrap space, a bulletin board displays favorite sewing items like vintage buttons (her personal weakness), threaded needles (at the bottom) and pins. Other notions are stored in glass jars on her bookshelf.

Accessibility is crucial to Rebecca's creative process. If an idea strikes to sew on a button, she no longer has to search for a button and threaded needle—she plans ahead: if she's already threading one needle, she'll thread three more so they're handy the next time.

Expert Tips from TRACY WHITE

"I used to keep tiny accents like eyelets and mini brads in watchmaker tins, but I recently made the switch to a new method, one that increases the manageability and amount of pieces I store. Now I group everything in Cropper Hopper Embellishment Essentials boxes that are simple to fill, label and collect within the Embellishment Essentials Organizer—a compact, portable system."

Q&A

Q: Whenever I find a way to store one type of accent, another product comes out that doesn't fit. How can I incorporate these new items without buying new containers?

A: Try storing your items in wire baskets—you can then hang extra items from the sides of the baskets with ribbon, beaded chains, S-hooks, binder rings or the original product packaging.

If you run into this dilemma frequently, you may want to try some open storage options instead. Use large wire baskets, canvas bins or drawer units, separating smaller items inside using jars, baskets or drawer dividers. If a larger item comes along, it can sit inside the big container, or you can just purchase another little basket instead of an entirely new storage unit.

Q & A

Q: Removing accents from packaging saves a lot of space, but what if I need to remember the product name or manufacturer?

A: When you're sure you'll need to recall product details (such as for supply lists), consider keeping packages intact—just find a storage system to house the extra bulk. If your space requires you to conserve space instead, try one of these ideas:

- Tear off package tops to store with the items—or insert handmade labels with the products as memory triggers.

- Snap quick snapshots of new purchases before you toss the packaging. Keep all the photos in a folder on your computer, sorted by the type of product for quicker searches.

- Log manufacturer and product descriptions in a notebook or section of your idea file.

- If all else fails, browse through Internet scrapbook shopping sites or your local scrapbook store to uncover the manufacturer names.

Expert Tips from LEAH LaMONTAGNE

"I organize small embellishments in a stackable storage system by LoRan—the Big Caddy. Each container features five compartments that open individually, and the containers stack to save space. I don't really have to come up with a way to sort the accents since I can find what I need just by looking at the stack."

SHARING SUPPLY-STASH EXTRAS

It's natural to want to sift through your growing supply stash (especially when your scrap space is too overcrowded to find anything!), but it can be difficult to actually get rid of the things you no longer want. Make it easier on yourself—remember that one person's trash is another's treasure. Don't toss your remnants—donate, trade or sell them instead. Try one of the following:

■ SWAPS. Set up a "supply switch" party with friends, or offer your items on the swap section of a scrapbooking message board. You can get some new goodies you've had your eye on as a trade for the items you no longer use.

■ SALES. Have a garage sale. Or check with your local scrapbook store—many host customer sales events or sell products for customers on a consignment basis.

■ DONATIONS. Charitable organizations, children's hospitals, schools, youth groups and community centers are always in need of supplies. You're sure to find it easier to part with your products when they go to a great cause.

■ GIFTS. A box of scrapbooking supplies is a smart way to get friends hooked on scrapbooking! Compile a "starter kit" for a friend who seems interested.

■ HAND-ME-DOWNS. If you've got "junior crafters" rifling through your stuff, label bins with their names and fill with scraps, extras and items you no longer want. Then they can scrap alongside you while you enjoy some creative time.

Tidy Tinys by BRITNEY MELLEN

Keep tiny embellishments tidy with a do-it-yourself drawer divider. When it's not tucked away in a drawer, this pretty tin serves as a colorful desktop addition!

WHAT TO GATHER:

☐ Cardstock (multiple colors)

☐ Circle punch (2")

☐ Muffin pan

☐ White metal spray paint

Supplies *Cardstock:* Die Cuts With a View; *Spray paint:* Krylon; *Other:* Muffin pan.

HOW-TO:

① Spray muffin pan with white metal spray paint.

② Use a 2" circle punch to create cardstock circles. Once paint has dried, drop a cardstock circle into each muffin-pan opening.

③ Sort small embellishments by color and place them into corresponding muffin-pan openings.

{CHAPTER 14}

ribbon, fibers
& embroidery floss

Ribbon, Fibers & Embroidery Floss

Is there anything more **colorful** and **pretty** than a pile of vibrant, textured **ribbon**? (A pile that isn't one gigantic knot, that is!) Keep your **gorgeous** stash of loose and **spooled ribbon**—in addition to pieces and cards of fiber, **embroidery floss** and beaded chains—in accessible **storage** that guards against tangling, **unraveling** and wrinkling. And of course, these **ideas** make sure they look good, too!

- ☐ Beaded chains
- ☐ Embroidery floss (loose and on cards)
- ☐ Lace
- ☐ Ribbon (loose, spools and on cards)
- ☐ Rickrack
- ☐ Twill tape

Sorting by Color

As soon as you turn the corner in the scrapbook store, it hits you—the rich, luxurious colors of the ribbon aisle. How can you resist? By the yard or by the spool, you most likely purchase ribbon based on its color.

Keep the vivid hues together by storing it the same way. Thread spools onto a dowel rod or place in a dispenser in "ROY G BIV" order—or in whatever arrangement makes you happy. If a length or spool features multiple colors, consider slotting it by:

- **Most dominant color**—What's the first shade you notice?

- **Background**—Ignore the polka dots; what color is the base?

- **Design**—Ignore the base; what color are the polka dots?

- **Compatibility**—What color will you most likely use it with?

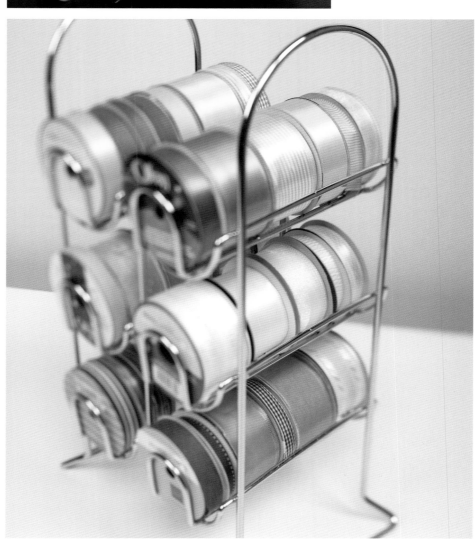

Sorting by Texture and Finish

What can be even more appealing than the color of ribbon? The feel. Delicate sheers, smooth satins, ridged grosgrains, soft twill tapes and more—if you purchase pieces based on their texture and finish, why not store them accordingly? When gathering materials for a layout, you might choose a specific look to reinforce the tone of your layout or a specific thickness to lend itself to a particular application. Some examples? Twill tapes can be torn and frayed, sheers can be strung through small holes to hang charms or act like "laces" through eyelets, sturdy grosgrains can be woven into borders, and wide satins can be stamped with solvent ink.

When storing by criteria such as texture, manufacturer or width, lean toward clear containers like cookie jars, open displays or wide-top units like baskets or wood bins that also allow you to see and select the proper color.

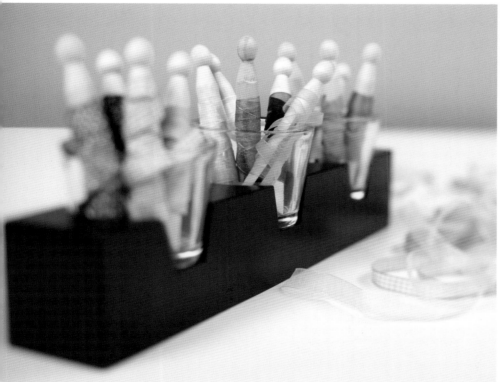

Sorting by Packaging

Unless you're willing to unroll all of your spools and cards of ribbon or are willing to roll loose pieces onto spools or cards, you'll need to devise storage systems to accommodate the different styles of ribbon, fiber and embroidery floss packaging. Each one has its advantages. Pieces can be compacted into small containers, cards can be stacked and flipped through, and spools are easy to hang and dispense. But just because they're kept in separate containers doesn't mean they can't sit together—group several ribbon-storage units on the same shelf or within the same section of your space. Bear in mind the different ways each can be housed:

• Pieces—Place in biscuit jars, spice canisters, punched paint cans and embellishment boxes; wrap on floss cards or clothespins; hang on hangers or clips.

• Spools—Store on dowel rods or paper-towel holders; place in baskets, boxes, ribbon organizers and dispensers.

• Cards—Hang on S-hooks, cup hooks or pegboards; house in mini albums, photos boxes and 3" x 5" index-card files.

Or use a system that allows both, such as S-hooks hanging on a metal shelf that holds spools. Rods for spools can be grouped with a pouch for cards. If you have a hanging set of rods, try clipping cards to the bottom rod using jump rings.

Expert Tips from BRENDA ARNALL

After experimenting with several different ways to organize pieces of ribbon, Brenda Arnall now stores lengths on small chipboard floss cards within plastic floss boxes. Here are her tips for making the system work:

- Separate cut lengths by color to make selection easier. Wrap pieces around cardboard "floss bobbins" (sold in most craft stores near the embroidery floss).

- Find plastic floss boxes with small compartments that keep ribbon manageable and prevent the other bobbins from falling over when one is removed.

- Store several boxes—one for each color family—together in a large basket.

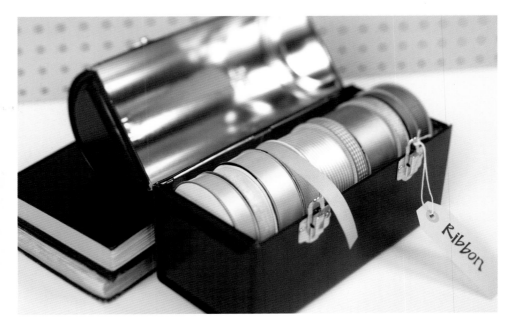

Q: Sorting ribbon by color is ideal for me, but what if I want to use product by a specific manufacturer on some layouts?

A: With some supplies, sometimes the best storage idea isn't a single system but a hierarchy of systems. Start with a main category, then divide that into a second or even a third. For example, if you primarily sort ribbon by color, subdivide within the color categories to create smaller batches based on your second selection system—whether it's by manufacturer, design, finish, width or type. Follow this multisystem idea for other supplies, such as patterned papers, accents and stamps as well.

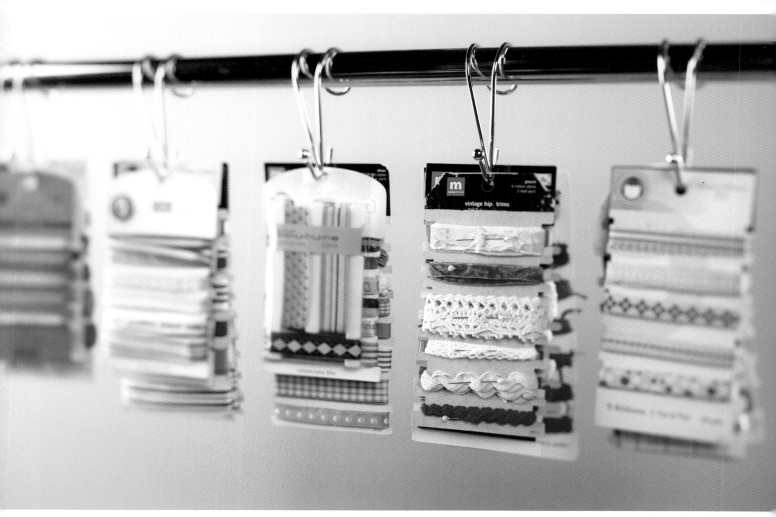

STORING FABRIC
AND SEWING NOTIONS

It's easy to integrate other craft techniques—such as sewing or stamping—onto your layouts, and it's even easier to incorporate the specialized supplies into your stash. For sewing products, try these ideas:

- Reserve a few drawers, files or pockets in your paper storage for fabric swatches.

- Use compartments in a plastic craft caddy or divided basket to hold thread, bobbins, needles and notions.

- Bring a traditional sewing box into your space—the layers and compartments are also great for fasteners and accents.

- Slip a needlework travel bag into your scrapbooking tote.

- Add chipboard inserts to vertical paper-storage holders to "hold up" larger pieces of fabric. Or simply stow colorful rolls of fabric in a basket or a bucket on a shelf.

- Use a "photo clutch" to hold smaller pieces of fabric, ribbon or trim.

Expert Tips from KELLY ANDERSON

"I know scrapbookers typically keep loose ribbon in clear glass biscuit jars, but I store my spools in them as well. They make it simple to locate everything, and they add color and a decorative touch to my room. My jars are available in three sizes, so they can hold a variety of spools."

Q & A

Q: Whenever I want to hand-stitch, I can find my embroidery floss but never my needle. How can I keep small items from getting lost in my stash?

A: Devise ways to put tiny pieces where they'll be impossible to lose. For example, store floss and thread in a closed metal tin. Place needles in a small box or vial with a strip of magnetic adhesive along the side, then "hang" it on the outside or top of the tin. Or save even more time—stick needles prethreaded with basic colors into a large pincushion, ready for sewing. The cushion can also hold decorative pins, eyelets or buttons threaded on long hatpins, or even remnants of ribbon or lace tacked down with a straight pin.

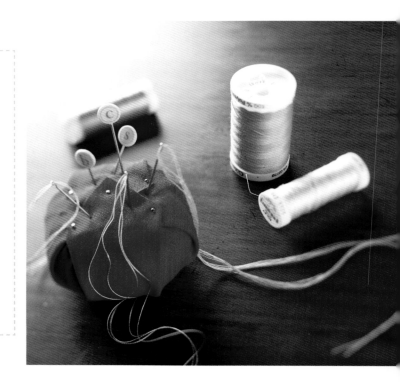

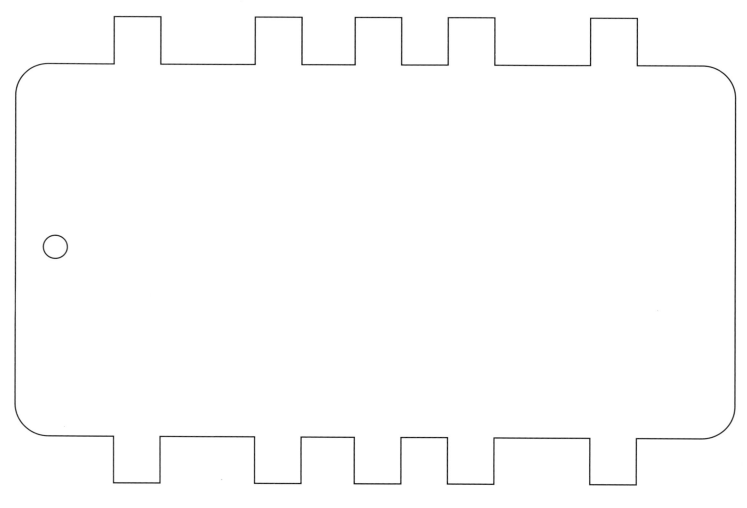

Ribbon Ring by BRITNEY MELLEN

Streamline your ribbon stash with these easy-to-make cards. String them on a key ring and find the right ribbon in a flash.

WHAT TO GATHER:

- ¼" hole punch
- Key ring or binder ring (purchased at an office-supply store)
- Ribbon card template (photocopy ribbon card template on page 240 at 100%)
- Scissors
- Straight pin or tape
- Thin cardboard

Supplies *Cardboard, straight pins, ribbons and key ring: Sources unknown.*

HOW-TO:

1. Trace template onto cardboard and cut out ribbon card.
2. Wrap ribbon strips around ribbon card and secure with a straight pin or tape.
3. Punch ¼" hole in the top of the card and thread onto key ring.

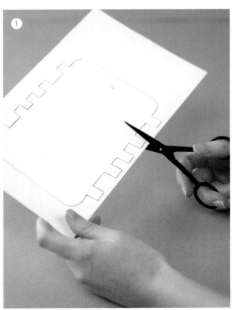

appendix

Packing for Crops

Ah, time for a crop—the opportunity for uninterrupted scrapping and socializing. But what should you take? If you don't pack enough, you may not be able to finish your project. If you take too much, you might spend more time sifting through totes than actually working. Plus, everything you pack has to be reorganized when you get home. How to simplify it? Think of the following when planning:

What to bring:

Ask the following questions to determine the amount of supplies you'll need to pack:

- **How long is the crop?** Think about how much time your typical project takes to complete, then determine how many layouts you can realistically fit into the session—especially when you'll spend time chatting with friends. If the crop is at a store, factor in the time you'll spend shopping as well.

- **What will be available at the crop?** If you're cropping in a store, you may be able to borrow larger tools.

- **Will you be socializing?** Pack materials to create smaller projects like cards or mini albums if you think you'll spend most of your time talking.

- **Can you finish later?** Take just the elements to get the basic page done—round corners, add accents or stamp designs at home.

- **Need a head start?** Don't spend time selecting materials at the crop. Assemble "page kits" before you leave home.

Where to put it:

If you need to purchase a tote to take along, consider such factors as:

- **SIZE.** Do you want to carry just the basics or the bulk of your stash? Will it be tucked away after the crop, or do you plan to use it as everyday supply storage?

- **COMPARTMENTS.** Are compartments roomy enough to slip smaller, prepacked containers into, or will you have to take the time to add accents and tools individually? Does it allocate the most room for the type of supply you use most—an open compartment for cardstock, for example, pockets for accents or even shelves for stamps?

- **PORTABILITY.** Are you taking a long walk from the car to the store? Will you need a telescoping handle and wheels, or will a shoulder strap do?

How to select it:

If you've organized your supplies following the four main sections in this book, pulling products for the crop will be a breeze. I use this method for gathering supplies from each zone:

INSPIRATIONS

1. Select batches of photos to include on specific layouts or within a mini album.

2. Slip the photos into a page protector and add any memorabilia for the page.

3. Add inspirational design, title or accent ideas that are clipped from magazines, sketched or written down.

FOUNDATIONS

1. Choose cardstock and patterned papers to coordinate with your selected photos. Stow them in an accordion file or poly envelope with a chipboard insert to prevent wrinkles.

2. If you want to work on cards, gather blanks and coordinating supplies in a file or box.

3. Save time at the crop—pack store-bought page kits or create your own (see the Kits chapter for tips on what to include).

CREATIONS

1. Slip basic tools—trimmer, scissors, pens, adhesives, rub-on tools and setters—into a supply pack or the loops of your bag. If you have an often-used tool caddy, just tote that outside your larger crop bag. Before you pack tools, check to see what large gadgets will be available to borrow at the crop. Coordinate with your friends as well, so you can share.

2. Complete backgrounds and accents with artistic media before the crop or after you get home. Purchase smaller sizes of inkpads that fit into tote pockets.

3. Pack only the alphabet and design stamps you'll need into tote pockets, a small envelope or an index-card file. Or stamp words beforehand that you can add to your page at the crop.

DECORATIONS

This is one zone where I try to take only the items I'll need, so I don't always take product from each storage section. But here's how I select the items I *will* take:

1. Take a plastic bag filled with coordinating sheets or loose letters to complete titles or monogrammed accents.

2. Include a small accordion file or binder to hold any flat embellishments.

3. Dimensional embellishments, such as fasteners, beads, acrylic shapes, buttons and more, can be organized in a small stacking canister or embellishment box.

4. Bring just the lengths of ribbon you expect to use rather than packing the whole spool—you can always add more later, if necessary.

Scrap-Space Solutions

Not all of us have the luxury of a dedicated scraproom in our home. But for those who do, you know it takes a lot to keep a large space organized. No matter what size your space is, you can turn it into the spot just right for your creative mind. Here are top tips for organizing, maximizing and personalizing any space.

Tote Bag

With the sizes and designs of totes these days, they're the perfect "space" if you're just starting out, with room for everything from tiny accents to tools to 12" x 12" cardstock. When using one as your sole supply storage, consider the following:

1. If you foresee the chance to expand, purchase your tote from a manufacturer that also makes units to stack on top. When not in use, conceal the tote beneath your desk, behind a chair or in a closet.

2. Don't waste space by filling the tote with containers. Find one that has pockets and dividers to hold items safely, and with enough room for your favorite type of scrapbook supply.

3. Store tiny embellishments in containers with secure-locking lids. You don't want to clean them up if the tote falls over.

4. Prevent product damage by not overfilling your bag. Once compartments are packed, vow to use or purge some of your stash before shopping again.

5. Even totes can reflect your personality and style—embellish them with tags or ribbon ties, which will also help you identify your bag when attending a convention or a crop.

Scrapbooking Armoire

What looks like a basic piece of furniture is actually a high-capacity spot to store your supplies. If you have the space for a scrapbooking armoire, increase what it will include with these five suggestions:

1. Opt for an armoire without a built-in work surface and position the unit near your dining room table, kitchen counter or even your living room floor—wherever you like to create. You'll have more room for supplies and will only have to take a few steps to reach them.

2. Sacrifice "cute" for efficient. Find practical, stackable containers to store more compactly—once the doors of your armoire are closed, no one will see them anyway.

3. Add nails to the inner walls to hang ribbon, tools and products on binder rings. Or cover the inside doors with magnets or pegboards to accommodate additional hooks, metal baskets and clips for small supplies or inspirational ideas.

4. Find kitchen-pantry organizers, wire racks or over-the-door pockets to house bulky tools, containers of embellishments or products kept in packaging.

5. Like tote-bag storage, an armoire will fill quickly if you buy too much and use too little. Sift through your stash regularly to eliminate items you'll never use.

Closet

From a bathroom cabinet to a spacious walk-in, a closet space gives you a spot of your own without sacrificing much "living space." Make it even more advantageous with ideas like these:

❶ Use existing closet rods to hold supplies hung on ribbon or binder rings, clipped in pant or skirt hangers, draped on tie or scarf racks, or stowed in hanging organizers.

❷ Make use of what you have—wall space. Install shelves from floor to ceiling or add pegboards to open spots. Even the wall behind hanging units can hold slim products, mesh bins and tins affixed to a magnet board.

❸ Use the back of the door to hang over-the-door accessory pouches, a wire CD/DVD rack or towel rods as out-of-the-way storage.

❹ Brighten a dark space with a lively color of paint, natural-light lamps safely secured or halogen strips installed below shelves. A mirror positioned to reflect a light source can "open it up," too.

❺ A closet space doesn't have to be a boring space. Add decor to increase personality— apply wall quotes, display favorite photos or hang an inspiration board.

Shared Space

Most every home has a niche collecting knickknacks or a corner collecting dust. Why not claim it as your own? A shared space lets you consolidate supplies and work near your family. To keep a living area from becoming cluttered, however, consider these tips:

❶ Find a work surface like a butcher-block kitchen island, card table or bed tray that can roll, fold up or slide out of the way when not in use.

❷ Use existing furniture as storage—think bookshelves, china cabinets, wall units or the cubby under the television.

❸ Make use of vertical space with tall drawer units, stacking crates and boxes or wall-mounted shelves.

❹ If space is at a premium, consider placing supplies you rarely use in clear bins stashed in the closet or under the bed in another room.

❺ If you're using your formal dining room table as a work surface, cover it with butcher-block paper, a self-healing cutting mat or a desk blotter when you scrap to protect it.

❻ If you'll be scrapbooking in another room, put together an often-used supply caddy to transport necessities back and forth.

❼ Gather "page kits" into a basket. Having photos, cardstock, paper and accents ready will allow you to scrapbook in spurts whenever you can sneak off to your space.

❽ Create a system to store pages-in-progress if your family uses your "work surface" at other times or if you're worried about little fingers "altering" your work. Or design on a large tray or self-healing mat you can move up or away when you're not around.

❾ Ensure a little privacy with a folding screen that conceals your mini studio.

❿ Keep the area tidy if your family complains or if it will be visible to guests. Don't let supplies, scraps or piles take over.

Dedicated Room

Whether it's your basement, a small guestroom or a lavish custom-designed space, a dedicated studio gives you the opportunity to infuse your own style from the ground up. Make it useful—and yours—with the following tips:

1. Design the space around your desk. Would you prefer to sit or stand? Look for a desktop deep enough to hold containers, tilt bins or drawer units along the back to keep often-used tools and supplies within reach when you work.

2. If your desk is small, don't pile everything on it. Set up stations throughout the room instead—one for page creation, another for your computer, a third for your sewing machine, die-cutting tools and so on.

3. Can't find the desk, shelving unit or container you're looking for? Try building it yourself. Ask around at a home-improvement store for suggestions and assistance.

4. Create a "flow" for your room that will make scrapbooking sessions more productive. Store supplies in an order that reflects how you typically select page materials—cardstock and paper, then embellishments, then tools and so on, such as the organization of the sections and chapters in this book.

5. Keep your supplies as visible as possible. Make use of open shelving, clear containers and pegboards or magnet boards . . . you may forget to use what you don't see.

6. If you prefer everything neatly tucked away, try not to stack items or containers more than two deep in drawers or cabinets. They'll be harder to reach and access—and if you don't want to make the effort, you may decide to cut them from your layout.

7. Use the closet to hold lesser-used supplies, surplus items or those you want doubly protected from sunlight and dust.

8. Decorate and motivate at the same time— display finished layouts and albums on shelves, in frames, on plate stands or in baskets.

9. Fill the room with what you love. If you enjoy travel, for example, find decorative containers, posters and other items that evoke memories of your favorite destinations—and that will inspire you when you sit down to create!

10. Be free! Make the space totally you—splash the walls with favorite colors, add quirky quotes, keep it neat or make a mess. Remember, you can always shut the door!

Index of Tips

Source Guide

Wonder *where* my team and I found all these great containers? We thought you might! So, we've *compiled* this list just *for* you. If a certain store isn't close to *home*, search online. Or simply check out your local kitchen, *office*-supply, craft or *home*-*decor* store for a similar item! *Enjoy*!

Book Cover

Contents

Photos

Memorabilia

Technology

Artistic Materials

Stamps

Letter Accents

Flat Embellishments

Dimensional Embellishments

Ribbon, Fibers & Embroidery Floss

Appendix

Thanks to the following companies that donated product to prop the organization containers in this book: 7gypsies, American Crafts, BasicGrey, Bazzill Basics Paper, Bo-Bunny Press, Cross-My-Heart, Darice, Fancy Pants Design, Heidi Swapp for Advantus, Karen Foster Design, KI Memories, Maya Road, me & my BIG ideas, and Pebbles Inc.